Nancy,

With love &
best wishes

Xmas 1986.   Marjorie

BRYANSTON
picture of a family

Frontispiece. **Sir William Portman: Lord Chief Justice of England.** [Died 1555.]
He acquired the London estate in 1553.

BRYANSTON
picture of a family

Marjorie Portman

dpc

DORSET PUBLISHING COMPANY
KNOCK-NA-CRE, MILBORNE PORT,
SHERBORNE, DORSET DT9 5HJ

Publishing details. First published 1987.
Text copyright Marjorie Portman © 1987.

Printing credits. Designed and published by Rodney Legg. Photography from Mrs Portman's collection
.   by Martin Farquharson of Farquharson and Murless, Poole, with the help of Jill Johnson.
Typeset by Santype International Ltd at Salisbury.
Printed in Great Britain by Wincanton Litho, Wincanton, Somerset, with platemaking by Andrew Johnstone
and machining by Steve Taylor.

Distribution. Trade sales distribution by Dorset Publishing Company from Knock-na-cre, Milborne Port, Sherborne, Dorset DT9 5HJ, telephone 0963 32583 or 0963 33643.

International standard book number (ISBN) 0 902129 88 0

For
Michael

Introduction

THE OLD kitchens and stables of Bryanston, the little eighteenth century church in the dark yew wood, the unchanging hills and meadows, the river and the beech woods; these tangible links possessed and loved, handed down from generation to generation, have been the inspiration for this book. It is the story of the Berkeley Portmans, who lived at Bryanston in the eighteenth century, written for their descendants who live today on the few remaining acres of the Bryanston estate still in the possession of the family.

In the years between, many who loved and cared for Bryanston, and brought up their children to do so, will be but lightly touched on. It would be impossible to bring to life so many generations of Portmans between the covers of one book. They would undoubtedly find such proximity in overcrowded conditions highly disagreeable and the writer would soon have to give up the unequal struggle of controlling their temperaments. I hope, however, that the children and grandchildren of Michael, who is of the seventh generation to live with his family in Dorset and fears he may be the last, will enjoy meeting Henry William—the only son of the first. They may find themselves in sympathetic company and perhaps even be grateful to those who forged the links which bind them and kept the chain unbroken for three hundred years.

1 The Duke in the ditch

ON A warm evening a small company of horsemen, riding wearily over a Dorset hill, drew rein and halted with relief at a command from their Captain. A few trees offered a welcome shade of which men and horses were not slow to take advantage. The Captain beckoned to his servant, who immediately brought his horse alongside his master's.

"Tis but a step now Matt, the road descends all the way to the valley of the Stour, and Blandford town where we will lie tonight, is no more than a mile or so by the river path. We shall find my Lord Lumley there, he may have gathered some information."

I do hope you be right Zur", Matthew replied, forgetting for the moment his soldierly status as he pushed back his hat to mop his sweaty face.

"Tis a sight too hot for chasin', glad I'll be when tis done".

"Have no fear Matthew, I'll warrant we take him before noon tomorrow." replied the Captain.

"Do I warn the lads Sir William? Glad they'll be to know food and lodging is near to."

His master nodded assent, and Matthew wheeled his horse smartly, too smartly, raising a cloud of dust from the hardbeaten drovers track. The Captain moved out of it and away from his men onto the open down.

Although so near the end of the long day's ride, he appeared in no hurry to proceed immediately. A cool breeze had sprung up on the hill top and the men too were content to ease their sore buttocks in the saddle, wipe the sweat and dust from their faces and to allow their horses to nibble the grass and any succulent morsels they could find in this oasis on the Dorset hills.

They were all men of Somerset, and the soft burr of their voices, the jingle of bits and bridles and the gentle blowing and munching of their mounts were the only sounds to reach the Captain. It was a musical accompaniment rather than a disturbance to the peace and beauty of the summer evening, as their Captain looked about him.

On his right he could see almost the whole of the smooth domed top of Hod Hill, brooding benevolently over the valleys, looking like a giant cottage loaf. The contours of the ancient fortifications, though clearly visible, gave little hint of the impregnable stronghold it once had been. The deep encircling ditches hewn out of the flint and chalk and the cunning traps designed to catch and maim the unwary invader who ventured so far, were now silted in and covered with a green mantle of grass.

Beyond, through a widening gap in the hills, he could see over the vale of Blackmoor to the distant Mendips and on his left some few miles along the valley, the church spire and huddled roof tops of Blandford. To this town, his immediate objective, the Captain paid little heed. His eyes and attention were caught and held by the valley below, where the sun glinted here and there on the river meandering through the water meadows, the white water of a mill race sparkled and danced invitingly in the sunlight. Steep wooded slopes, gentle coombs and the rounded hills rising from the valley, looked so clear in the evening light, that it seemed possible to stretch out a hand and ruffle the leaves of the trees and with one finger to trace the line of a narrow white road which climbed straight to the top of the highest hill.

As he gazed a new enchanted sound attracted his attention. For a moment he was at a loss to identify it. And then he saw them. Seven swans in dignified effortless flight on their way down the river.

They seemed to put the final seal on the curiously intimate and friendly charm of this place, with its air of being lived in and loved for longer than man could remember.

The year was 1685 and Sir William Portman, Baronet, Knight of the Bath, Member of Parliament and Captain of Militia, holding a commission empowering him to march his Company into any of the Western counties, was engaged on an important assignment. His militiamen were seeking the rebel Duke of Monmouth who, thanks to his misguided friends, had lately fought and fled defeated from the battle of Sedgemoor. However, from Sir William's point of vantage on the hill, he was not only concerned with possible suspicious movements below; it was the beauty of the valley itself which occupied most of his attention.

History relates that Sir William's mission was successful, for early on a Wednesday morning, 8 July 1685, he discovered the Duke hidden in a ditch beneath a pile of leaves and bracken under an ash tree in the parish of Woodlands, at the edge of Horton Heath, ten miles east from Blandford. The Duke would have been shot on the spot if Sir William had not restrained his men. Some years before he had bought the Bryanston property from the heirs of Richard Rogers. If there was any special reason for Sir William doing so it has been obscured by time and can only be a matter of speculation. It is possible, however, that born during the Civil War, and growing up under the Protectorate among people who loathed the regime and lived only for the day when a Stuart should be restored to the throne, William, the orphaned son of a staunch Royalist, would have been deeply interested in stories of the war and of his father's part in it, which could not have been inconsiderable, for Cromwell saw fit to mulct the boy's estate of £25,000.

In October 1644, the month of young William's birth, his father was with Charles and his Court at Bryanston, guests of the widowed Anne Rogers, whose husband Richard had died in 1643 after his gallant attempt to take Sherborne for the King. The King's regiment of Horse Guards were quartered in the nearby village of Durweston, with Prince Maurice's army higher up the river at Sturminster. There was a great rendezvous on Durweston Down. It was a time when Royalist hopes were high. Sir John Berkeley, later Lord Berkeley of Stratton, had succeeded in consolidating the West and with this new strength victory for the King's forces seemed at last to be in sight.

To a lonely boy whose only knowledge of his father came from the stories retailed to him by family retainers, these events which took place shortly before his father's death must have been of particular interest. And at a time when a gentleman's servants served the same family from generation to generation, not only looking after his master's comforts in peace but also fighting beside him in war, the story would undoubtedly have been first hand, though spiced with the colour, embroideries and elaborations which are inevitable when stories are told and retold, until they become delightful and romantic legends. It is not difficult to imagine that for this reason from his earliest boyhood, Bryanston might have held a special magic for young William and that he finally fell completely in love with its beauty on that summer evening, when he in his turn was serving a Stuart king. He was a gentleman of considerable fortune and able to indulge his lightest whims. When his father died, in 1645, William was scarcely one year old. As the only surviving male of his line, he inherited the large family estates in Somerset, and with them the baronetcy, for though his father was but the fourth son of Sir John—created a baronet in 1612—the three elder brothers, Henry, John and Hugh, though inheriting each in their turn, all died without issue.

The family had been known in Somerset for more than four hundred years, holding lands there in the reign of Edward I. If these were not originally so extensive, his ancestors had rectified this by good husbandry, and by their sagacity and forethought in frequently marrying their sons to the heiresses of neighbouring estates. The tradition of his family had always been one of service to their King and Country and if, through the years, they had gained great riches, these were not only well deserved but well dispensed. They showed no greed for power nor desire to intrigue in high places.

William's most famous ancestor was Sir William Portman, Lord Chief Justice of England in the reign of Henry VIII, who continued in that office through Philip and Mary's troubled reign. "In which situation," it was said of him, "he distinguished himself by displaying a degree of integrity and independence very unusual among the judges of those arbitary and despotic times."

For the most part William's family had been content to look after their tenants, serve their country as members of Parliament and to serve their King as and when required to do so, and had generally displayed that same integrity which made the Judge remarkable.

After the Civil War, when this proud heritage reposed solely in the person of one small boy, it was inevitable that from an early age William should have been made aware not only of his wealth, privileges and potential importance, but also of the great responsibilities which rested on his young shoulders. Not the least of these was the vital necessity of producing an heir.

Child betrothal was the custom of the age, and William's guardians lost no time in arranging for him a suitable marriage. He was betrothed to Elizabeth, daughter of Sir John Cutler, almost as soon as he was breeched. In spite of this early start in the matrimonial field, for the marriage was confirmed and consumated as soon as the children reached their teens, William's bride was to die childless before he was thirty. He very soon married again, another Elizabeth, daughter of Sir John Southcott, and undaunted by her demise within seven years, he took yet a third, Mary, daughter of Sir John Holman of Northamptonshire. Newly married to Mary, at the time of the Monmouth rebellion, and comparatively young, he must still have had hopes of getting his heir. However, in less than three years Mary too was dead.

All William's wives were heiresses in their own right and his marriages must have considerably increased his fortune, but not one of them could give him the treasure he most desired, a son to succeed him and make certain the continuation of his line, which now appeared to have come to an end.

William's pride of family was shown by his determination, that in spite of nature's unkind lack of co-operation his estates should still remain intact and in the ownership of a family with Portman blood in its veins and bearing his name.

By a deed dated February 1689, just a year after Mary's death and a few months before his own, at only 45, he devised his estates to Henry Seymour, his cousin, on condition that he took the name and arms of Portman.

Henry was the fifth son of William's guardian, Sir Edward Seymour, and his aunt Anne, his father's eldest sister. From the age of seven, when he lost his mother, he had been brought up in the Seymour household. The youngest of the Seymour brothers, only a few years his senior, must have been like a brother to the orphaned boy, and William undoubtedly had an affection for him which did not extend to his other cousins, whom he completely ignored in the other provisions of his will. In fact he took good care that his fortune should not be divided and dissipated by the Seymours, for in the event of Henry dying without issue, the estates were to go to the descendants of his father's other sister, Joan. This again would be on condition that they took the name of Portman.

It is interesting to reflect that but for Sir William's forethought, not only would his family have died out with him, but many London streets and squares would not proclaim today, by their familiar names, their link with Dorset and Somerset and with the family who owned those "golden" acres four hundred years ago. Strange too, that this unimportant property, in Middlesex, a few green meadows watered by the Tyburn brook, fit only for asses to graze, and oddly acquired by a Lord Chief Justice of England in exchange for a man's life, should become the source of the family's wealth when the rich estates in the West Country had become a liability. If, however, Sir William had died content, satisfied that he had assured the continuation of his name, it is as well he could not foresee the fragile thread on which it was to depend for the next hundred years.

2 To High Hall,
to seek a bride

SARAH GODWYN sewed rapidly, the truckle bed beside her was heaped with feminine garments, all needing repair, new laces or new ribbons.

The afternoon was hot and she had opened both the door and the tiny window over the sun-splashed yard in an attempt to cool the cubby hole in which she worked.

The house was quiet and except for the cooing of the pigeons there was for once no sound from the stables.

The drowsy silence was broken as a door opened below, and the murmur of voices drifted up to her, followed by the sound of running footsteps on the stairs. She wondered idly who could be so stupid as to race about in this heat. Then hearing her name called, she looked up from her work with a puzzled frown, surprised at the unaccustomed urgency in Anne's voice.

"Sarah",—yes it was Anne calling. Rising quickly she turned towards the open door, then stopped at the sound of a scuffle followed by a squeak of pain.

"So tis you Melody, get out, and send Sarah to me immediately. And hasten you prying wretch."

A door banged, and in a moment a print clad figure, topped by a large red face, appeared in the doorway. Breathing heavily, Melody's expression of hurt indignation was slightly upset by finding herself face to face with Sarah.

"Why there you be Sarey, did you not hear. She be calling you, and her be near to weeping I'd say, and in a mortal rage. When she found twas I in her chamber, catched me by the ear she did." Ruefully Melody rubbed her right ear which was indeed very slightly redder than the rest of her face.

"Never did I see her in such a taking, tis not like our Anne. With the Mistress now, I know when to duck, see."

Sarah cut her short. "Then you had better duck now, before I'm minded to catch you by the other." She pushed the girl aside, and hurried down the passage, alarmed and surprised by her young mistress's unusual behaviour.

Anne, unlike most of her family, never raised her voice, rarely demanded a service, and was always calm, placid and kind.

Drawing no attention to herself, she contrived to move quietly through the life of High Hall like an efficient, friendly ghost.

She was standing near the window, her back to the room as Sarah entered. A slim, tall figure outlined against the light. Without turning she spoke.

"Sarah? What was that misnamed imbecile doing in here?"

"Poor Melody? No harm I think." Sarah glanced round the prim, neat room. Everything was as usual in its appointed place. Anne had but lately been allowed a bedchamber of her own, having previously shared one with her sisters, and was inordinately jealous of the privacy it had given her. Only Sarah was permitted to come and go as she pleased. Quietly, in her own way, Anne had made this clear to the rest of the household.

Sarah had been employed at High Hall since she was twelve years old. Pretty, intelligent, the orphaned child of Quaker parents, brought up by them to be industrious, diligent and God-fearing, she had soon been promoted from sewing maid to personal attendant to William Fitch's daughters, all of whom now regarded her more as a friend than as a servant. Anne, particularly, had a special affection for her, and discovering that the child could already read and write a little, and finding her a more interesting companion than her own frivolous sisters, had shared and passed on the little education she herself had been lucky enough to acquire. Now she turned impatiently to the girl.

"Yes, yes, no matter. Sarah, what am I to do?" Her eyes shining with anger were enormous in her small face, pale as always, but on her mouth was the hint of a mutinous pout, which Sarah had never seen before.

With a sense of surprise Sarah realised that her mistress was beautiful. Certainly she had never looked more so than now in this strange mood. Gone the lowered lids, the placid mask in repose. Even the characteristic droop of her thin shoulders was missing. This was a strange, new Anne, and Sarah was at a loss to account for the change. Uncertainly she moved towards her mistress.

"My dear, what in the world is amiss?"

"Do *you* not know, is it possible that Mama has resisted the temptation to boast to *you* of the success of her schemes. No, of course, she would fear that they would be revealed to me, and that I might find a way to defeat her aims, as with time indeed I should have done." She paced restlessly up and down the room, and went on bitterly. "All these months she has been big with her secret plans. What pain it must have been for her to keep them to herself—and I, poor fool, thought twas all forgotten. I am to be married,"

She flung the bare statement at Sarah, as if no further explanation of her distress was necessary. In the silence that followed, these last words seemed to lie between them, tangible as a gauntlet thrown down in challenge. Any comforting cliches which might have risen to Sarah's lips died unspoken in the face of Anne's misery, which could not have been greater if she had announced that she was to die.

Bewildered and uncomprehending Sarah turned away and carefully rearranged the folds of the drapery round the bed.

Who was this monster to whom poor Anne was betrothed? Mistress Fitch had surely guarded her secret well for Sarah knew of no suitor so horribly offensive as this future bridegroom appeared to be, to Anne. In a moment, the maid found the courage to enquire his name.

Anne answered in a flat expressionless voice, as if it was of no consequence.

"He is Mr. Portman of Bryanston."

"A Mr. Portman," Sarah exclaimed in surprise, "how very odd. Did not your sister Meliora go first as a bride to Bryanston, many years ago, to a husband old enough to be her grandfather?"

She stopped, aghast, thinking for one moment that she understood. Had they found another ancient widower of this same rich family, to whom they would sacrifice yet another daughter on the altar of Mistress Fitch's pride and ambition.

No, there must be another explanation, but Anne was silent and volunteered nothing further.

Meliora's marriage had taken place long before Sarah came to High Hall but she had heard from others of the scenes, tears and tantrums which had followed the announcement of the seventeen year old girl's betrothal to a widower already long past seventy. However, she knew too, that Meliora was enough like her mother to finally appreciate the advantages of becoming the Mistress of Bryanston and Orchard Portman and that her husband had not survived long enough to spoil too many of her youthful years, nor her chances of marrying again. Anne, however, was quite different. Even the ambitious Mistress Fitch could hardly contemplate forcing a similar marriage on her. Fastidious, sensitive, no longer a child but a woman with a mind of her own, it would be monstrous. Anne was, moreover, William Fitch's favourite, and gentle and kindly as he was, he would surely never allow his wife to have her way this time.

Sarah wished Anne would speak, tell her more. She was completely at a loss and more puzzled than ever. Unable to bear the silence and tension any longer, impulsively she went to Anne and put her arms around her.

"Do not distress yourself so," she begged. "You can rest assured you will not be forced, your father would never allow it. He loves you dearly and is a great deal too kind to insist you marry someone so abhorrent to you."

Anne pushed her away almost violently.

"You do not understand, no one understands."

She sank down on the bed, looking up at Sarah with wide, stormy eyes, allowing the unchecked tears to race unheeded down her cheeks to fall like rain drops, leaving small dark smudges on her gown. Sarah had never seen anyone cry like that before and in spite of her concern she was fascinated. Instead of the soggy red-eyed mess it made of most people's faces, Anne's tears only seemed to increase her beauty.

"I hate them," her mistress went on, "all of them, with their drinking, and wenching, foul-mouthed, stinking of sweat. I'd rather die than have to submit to one of them." She thumped the bed with her small fist. "I do not wish to share my room or my bed, to be pawed and handled and made to bear horrible children. I don't want to marry anyone," she finished with a wail, and flung herself down on the pillows weeping uncontrollably.

It was quite extraordinary and revealed to Sarah a facet of Anne's character which before she had but rarely glimpsed. Nevertheless, this unexpected exhibition of passionate revolt against marriage did explain many things which had sometimes puzzled the girl. It explained why Anne had taken so much trouble to make herself indispensable to her mother in the running of the household. This suited Mistress Fitch admirably, preferring, as she did, a life of visits, gossip and playing cards with her neighbours, and the planning of new gowns, to tedious chores and worrying about what the stillroom maids were getting up to. Quietly and efficiently Anne had freed her mother from all such tiresome matters. To her father also she had made herself almost indispensable, sharing his love of books and music, anticipating and providing everything for his comfort. And in her quiet company he was accustomed to find a welcome refuge from his wife's clattering tongue.

It explained, too, why Anne had left the field clear for her younger sisters when any possible suitor appeared. Keeping in the background, always too busy to join in their frivolous games; dressing so simply that she was sometimes taken for a waiting woman and rarely giving a visitor an opportunity to observe that she was by far the prettiest of the three daughters.

Sarah was intelligent, but although she now saw clearly the purpose of Anne's behaviour, the reason for it was puzzling. In those days long before the advent of the psychiatrist, older and wiser heads than hers would not even have bothered to search for it, though perhaps it was really not so hard to find. For at the time of Meliora's betrothal, Anne, still a small child, had witnessed the battle between her mother and sister which had raged noisily for weeks through the house. Too young to understand or to be told of the gross unsuitability of the match, the sensitive, gentle child grew up with the fixed idea that the marriage state was too horrible to contemplate and a fate to be avoided at all cost. Nor in later years did her mother, with her constant vulgar allusions to love in or out of matrimony, together with pious instruction to her younger daughters on the duties of a woman to please her husband in all things, add anything at all to its attractions.

Sarah realised only that beneath Anne's gentle manner had lain concealed an iron hard determination which few people had suspected her of possessing and she had deliberately contrived for some unknown reason to remain unmarried. Now in her late twenties she must have thought she was safe. Only half understanding but sensing the bitterness of her mistress's defeat, Sarah stood by helplessly, hoping that this second Mr. Portman to come seeking his bride at High Hall would at least not prove to be quite so advanced in years as the previous one.

Anne rose hastily at the sound of voices and the crisp rustle of many petticoats approaching her door. She threw an agonised glance at Sarah who could do no more than momentarily shield Anne from view as her mother and sisters unceremoniously invaded the room. Sweeping past Sarah as though she did not exist, Mistress Fitch advanced on her daughter.

"Tears, tears! My love, this will not do," she cried as she embraced her. "And here I have brought Kate and Mary to wish you happiness and rejoice with you my child, on your good fortune."

"I am not a child Mama, nor do I consider myself fortunate in this situation," Anne replied with spirit.

"Tut, tut, that is no way to talk, and your dear sisters near green with envy."

Catherine flushed, fully aware that this remark was directed at herself alone, and was quick to reply.

"Why indeed it must be something of a shock to a person of Anne's sensitivity to be so suddenly swept into matrimony at her age. Whereas, I declare, our dear Mary, betrothed these two years to her Mr. Russell, has become so accustomed to the idea, she has the air of a married woman already, and by the time he at last gets his living, she will scarcely notice the trying formality of the marriage service."

Mary giggled, she could never untangle Catherine's complicated jibes and accepted them quite happily, as compliments, unaware of any malice concealed within them.

With a helpless glance at Anne's stony face, Sarah quietly left the room, unaccountably feeling sorry for Catherine who so desperately wanted a husband, and trying hard to repress a slight feeling of irritation with Anne. She did not return to her work, however, feeling a need for the open air and time to sort out her own thoughts, she slipped out of the house and down through the paddocks to the beech woods.

3 Mr. Berkeley stumbles upon Sarah

THAT SAME afternoon, a young man leading a horse, slowly made his way down a track northward from Badbury Rings. His clothes proclaimed him a gentleman not only of substance but of fashion; the cut of his coat spelt London and even the chalky white dust could not entirely obliterate the high shine and elegant fit of his boots besides which the quality of the mare he led so carefully was unmistakeable.

Inwardly cursing his decision to take the shorter way across the rings to High Hall, whilst insisting on his manservant continuing on the turnpike through Wimborne, he nevertheless trudged on patiently and made no attempt to hurry the mare who had stumbled and lamed herself as she cantered towards the earthworks across the apparently flat turf beside the high road. Hot and tedious as he found this unaccustomed foot-slogging across country nothing could have persuaded him to put a leg across the mare whom he not only valued highly but also held in great affection. Very soon, however, he reached the easier going of the flat meadows, and it was with considerable relief that he at last sighted the neat brickwork of High Hall perched on its little knoll not half a mile distant.

A few minutes later, skirting a beech coppice which now alone separated him from his destination, he was diverted by the unexpected appearance of a young woman who emerged suddenly from the covert some little way ahead of him. She had been running but on reaching the open ride she paused in full sunlight, flinging out her arms as if welcoming its brightness and warmth. Her white capped, grey clad figure was dwarfed by the tall beeches behind. For a moment she stood motionless, then with an odd defiant gesture snatched the cap from her head and flung it away, allowing a mop of red gold hair to tumble in unconfined abandon about her shoulders. With a quick shake as if to make certain that every strand should have its full freedom, she spun round, executed a spontaneous little dance and then flung herself full length on the springy turf in the shade of the overhanging trees which had successfully masked his own approach. Determined not to frighten away this "nymph"—who was obviously unaware of his presence—the stranger hitched the mare to a convenient branch

and continued alone more cautiously. The leaf laden trees and the
grassy track conspired with him, and he was almost beside her
when suddenly aware that she was no longer alone, the girl sat up
in some confusion. With incredible rapidity she made an attempt
both to re-arrange her skirts more modestly and to smooth back her
tumbled curls. Before she could rise to her feet however, the
gentleman was seated comfortably by her side.

"Pray do not disturb yourself," he begged. "You have chosen a
delightful place and with your permission ma'am, I am more than
pleased to share it with you."

Sarah stared at him in amazement, it was as if he had been
conjured out of the midsummer air in answer to her muddled
dreams. Young, well-looking and with a warm sparkle in his eyes
and a slightly rakish air which if to be deprecated, certainly added
to his attraction. He was the embodiment of all the romance she
could have wished, not only for Anne but indeed for herself. For
however hard she had tried to guide her thoughts sympathetically
to her Mistress's distress as she walked, her own strange feelings of
frustration and bitterness would obtrude themselves. Her sympathy for Catherine, she realised, was no more than a reflection of
her own self-pity. Who would marry either of them? Kate, with
her spiteful tongue, the eldest and plainest of the sisters; one of a
family with no great fortune or connections. She would be lucky
now to find an elderly person who needed a wife to keep house for
him. As for herself, a menial in that family, what chances had she
of ever leaving it and having her own establishment. Certainly no
help or dowry would she get from the Fitch's, occupied as they
were in finding husbands for their own daughters.

In her short life Sarah had had little time for thinking of herself or
of her own feelings and even in the welcome peace of the woods her
thoughts had been confused. The sudden prospect of change in
Anne's life and her strange reaction to it, had brought to the surface
emotions, hopes and fears which previously Sarah had repressed so
firmly that she had been hardly aware of their existence. As she
wandered on much further than she had intended, she had suddenly felt chill, the silence and gloom of the woods had become oppressive, frightening. She felt small, lost and alone, her one coherent
thought that there was really no-one in the whole world who really
cared what became of her. The grey trunks of the trees seemed to
menace her with their height and strength, and the leafy canopy
above, blotting out the sun, seemed to close in on her, a suffocating
trap from which there was no escape. On an impulse she had

picked up her skirts to blindly run down the ride towards the sunlight, more to escape her own thoughts than the sinister shapes of the trees, for the glimpse she had had of Anne's secret feelings that afternoon had badly cracked the veneer of the efficient, reliable servant which she herself had worn for so long, and all the desires and emotions of a rebellious teenage girl, greedy for life, were trying to break through. Her panic left her as she ran and was replaced by a sense of freedom, and joy in this unaccustomed exercise. At last out in the sunlight lying exhausted on the warm thyme scented grass, for a brief moment, before the arrival of the stranger, she was as relaxed and carefree as a child.

As Sarah stared incredulously at the man who had so unexpectedly joined her, he took off his hat and with a gesture very like her own of a few moments before, tossed it carelessly aside. Her eyes followed its course and she blushed as it came to rest beside her small white cap lying in the middle of the ride. So he had seen her run out of the woods and all her antics. Furiously she sat up straight gathering the shreds of her young dignity about her. As she turned to look at him she realised that he was not unknown to her.

"Why, tis Mr. Berkeley," she gasped, "what brings you here, and on foot?"

He bowed, "Your servant, ma'am. Twas not my intention I assure you," he indicated the mare with a wave of his hand. "Lame," he shrugged, "my own careless fault, for which I have paid dearly with a hot and tedious walk, but am rewarded by your charming presence and flattered that you should remember me for it is many months since I was at High Hall."

"Surely sir, I have good reason for doing so," Sarah replied tartly.

Recognition dawned suddenly in his eyes. "Indeed, yes, tis the lack of a cap which changes you. You were pretty enough with it, but without you are beautiful," he said, regarding her with renewed interest.

"Sir, you will understand that my very reason for remembering you prompts me to leave immediately."

"I beg you will not, please stay a while and you will find me a changed man and a model of propriety, though tis pleasing to know that my kisses . . ."

Sarah glared at him.

"Your pardon ma'am." Hastily he corrected himself. "That even my attempted kisses should be so long remembered."

You were at that time I think considered to be a suitor for one of Mistress Fitch's daughters." Sarah's voice was cold, but as she started to rise, Mr. Berkeley lazily reached out a hand, gently encircled her wrist and held it firmly down against the ground.

"How true. Your memory is formidable, but to be more specific it was Anne, I assure you. If one must marry one of the Fitch girls and for some strange reason my family were set upon it, it would have to be Anne. Do you not agree? She has a delicacy, an aristrocratic air which the others entirely lack."

He regarded her quizzically through half closed eyes. Lying back against a tree, he looked so relaxed and indifferent that Sarah made a quiet attempt to free herself, but found the grip on her wrist as firm as ever. She was not perturbed, she had a weapon which must undoubtedly disturb his complacency.

"Then I wonder what brings you to High Hall today Sir. For if you seek to renew your suit, I fear your journey is wasted."

"Surely not wasted, when I have the pleasure of meeting once more her lovely Abigail. But that aside, may I know the reason for your discouraging remark? Mistress Anne continues in good health I hope, she is not . . ." he paused and regarded Sarah with polite concern.

"My Mistress is in excellent health, Sir," Sarah replied shortly, "and is soon to be married."

Mr. Berkeley's reaction to this was disappointing.

Only one eyebrow was raised very slightly as he enquired casually, "To whom, may I ask, should I tender my congratulations? To Mr. Portman of Bryanston by any chance?"

"He is known to you Sir?" asked Sarah eagerly. Her companion nodded. "I am very well acquainted with him," he replied.

In her excitement and hope of getting some information about the unknown Mr. Portman she failed to notice that Mr. Berkeley's hands were now comfortably cushioning his head and that she was therefore free to rise and leave if she wished.

"Oh please, do tell me what you know of him. I fear he is not at all what my poor Anne would desire. I think it is a shame to force her. Is he very old? His looks, is he ill-favoured? Or worse is he a gambler and a rake? I know he is rich, for Mistress Fitch is so very happy about it all, and Bryanston I understand is a fine estate, but I cannot think why I have not heard of him before this time."

The words tumbled out, Sarah's cool and formal air quite forgotten as she sat hugging her knees, her eyes alight with interest, firing her questions at him, looking like an enchanting child begging for a story.

"Mr. Berkeley laughed out loud. "Enough, I will do my best to satisfy your curiosity, but one question at a time. Now age." He looked doubtful. "Well he is no longer a boy it is true."

"Over fifty?" asked Sarah with a worried frown.

"No—no indeed, I can safely say he is not over fifty. And as for looks how can I tell you what ladies consider ill or well favoured?"

"Oh dear, you are not so very helpful. You must have some notion. Now yourself for example. You are the right sort of age and as for looks," she regarded him thoughtfully for a moment. I do not wish to flatter Sir, but if you had continued with your suit I think she might have found you tolerable."

Mr. Berkeley bowed slightly as well as he was able in his recumbent position. "You are very kind ma'am. In that case I think Mistress Anne should be well satisfied with the Squire of Bryanston. I assure you he is no worse looking than myself, and by some ladies might even be considered to be moderately handsome."

Sarah sighed with relief, then shook her head despondently. "Tis not after all so simple. Though I own tis a consolation to know he is not what I feared. The truth is that my poor Mistress does not wish to marry anyone. She appears strangely to have set her heart on remaining in a single state."

Mr. Berkeley opened one eye, he appeared to be nearly asleep. "Do not distress yourself my dear. So far she has known no other," he drawled, "how can she know the joys of matrimony and motherhood until she has experienced them." Suddenly he sat up. "But wait, we have forgotten your last question. Reluctant as I am to answer it, I fear I must tell you that Mr. Portman is undoubtedly a gambler and there are those who are of the opinion that he is also something of a rake. Poor dear Anne. I remarked, I think, before on her delicacy, she will find that hard to bear. You must go with her to Bryanston, Sarah, and be her consolation. Come now I will escort you back to the house."

He leapt up, and reached out a hand to help her to her feet. For a moment they stayed hand in hand and very close. Looking up Sarah surprised an odd look on his face, but as she turned away he quickly released her and went off down the track to retrieve the mare. Thoughtfully Sarah smoothed her crumpled skirts, and brushed away a few clinging leaves. It had not occurred to her before that she might accompany Anne to her new home, but now the idea had been planted in her mind, she was determined to persuade Anne to take her. As they walked slowly towards the

BRYANSTON: PICTURE OF A FAMILY

house through the little park, Mr. Berkeley leading the mare, Sarah begged him to tell her more about Bryanston. Was it a great house? How many were there in the household? Was it far enough from the town to have escaped the dreadful fire which had completely destroyed Blandford a few years ago? He must tell her, please. It would be of advantage to her Mistress to know something of her future home. Mr. Berkeley once more patiently answered her questions. There was one however, which she longed to ask on her own account but did not do so directly. It was whether he himself was a close neighbour. Anyhow it proved unnecessary, for his replies convinced her that the answer to that was in the affirmative.

He described the beauties of Bryanston in detail, the gardens and the exceptionally fine plantations down the great riverside cliff which extended for about two miles from the manor house, to the old bridge at Blandford. He was interesting and amusing about the house itself. A medieval manor he told her, parts of it dating back to the thirteenth century, rambling, old fashioned and inconvenient besides being horribly damp owing to its proximity to the river. Nevertheless its situation was pretty enough, it required only a Mistress and a family to bring it to life again, and a master to spend money on making it more comfortable. One suggestion made her laugh. In all seriousness he proposed that Mr. Portman would be well advised to move the river a little further away from his door step. Then he refused to tell her more unless she consented to walk beside him, complaining that it was impossible to carry on a conversation if she persisted in staying on the other side of the mare where he could not even see her.

Sarah, however, assured him that she had already been too long absent from her duties and should hurry on ahead and warn the household of his coming. With a pat for the horse and a brief bob to himself she was gone, running lightly up the little rise to the house. Mr. Berkeley smiled with amusement as he watched her. He remembered very well his first visit to High Hall. Bored with the elder Fitch girl who so obviously set her cap at him and piqued by Anne's cool indifference he had been impatient to return to the freedom and sophistication of London. Yet his encounter with Sarah, on the third day, and the subsequent week of hide and seek he had played with her in an attempt to overcome her reluctance to accept his attentions had caused him to stay even longer than he had intended. Unsuccessful as he had been he could not but admit that she had a dignity, a charm unusual in a girl of her station, besides an elusive quality which had attracted him then and had haunted his thoughts for many weeks after he had returned to the easier pleasures of the town.

In the stable yard, as he left the mare in the hands of his waiting and worried servant, he glanced up and glimpsed Sarah at an open window. She smiled and waved gaily to him. So she did not yet know the truth. He wondered just how cross she was going to be when she realised how he had teased her.

4   Anne's resignation

SARAH WAS to discover very soon that Mr. Berkeley and the Squire of Bryanston were one and the same person. Summoned in haste by Anne to help her change her dress, she was surprised to hear that Mr. Portman was already below, and puzzled too when Anne went on to say that it would have been a great blessing if her mother's forebodings of the past hour had indeed come true! These appeared to be either that the gallant Squire had fallen from his horse and broken his neck or alternatively had had second thoughts about his bride and returned post-haste to Blandford.

"But why should Mistress Fitch have imagined such a thing?" Sarah asked casually, waiting only for an opportunity to speak of her own encounter with Mr. Berkeley and to retail to Anne what he had told her. Carefully arranging her Mistress's hair before the mirror and wishing that she would not look quite so unhappy and miserably resigned, Sarah scarcely heeded the reply to her question until a few words caught her attention . . .

". . . the horse went lame, and he was forced to walk. Though it is no more than two or three miles, he took a wondrous long time about it. His man was here fully an hour sooner, and was in as much of a tizzy as dear Mama."

Brush in hand Sarah paused and gazed incredulously at her Mistress's reflection. She opened her mouth to speak but checked herself. It was surely too much of a coincidence for two different gentlemen to have arrived on foot each leading a lame horse to High Hall that afternoon. Here was a mystery and Sarah determined to discover it before saying another word. With her thoughts elsewhere she was unusually slow and clumsy as she continued her task of dressing her mistress.

Finally Anne cried out in exasperation: "What ails you child. You are all thumbs. Hurry I beg you. I will be late and have vexed Mama enough for one day." Before she left the room, however, Anne turned back to Sarah with her usual gentle manner.

"You must forgive my impatience dear Sarah, this has been a monstrous horrid day for me, but I am resigned now to my fate, and must make the best I can of it."

She leant forward and kissed the girl lightly. "But you will come with me to Bryanston. I have begged Mama to allow it. For I fear my future husband is a sorry rake and has of little use for matrimony as I have myself. His only purpose is to get himself a son. Why, did not he try to force his odious attentions upon you when he was here before to ask for my hand."

Sarah hoping to have the position made quite clear looked more puzzled than she really felt, and Anne went on, "Yes, but he was of course known by the name of Berkeley then. You must surely recollect the gentleman."

"Yes indeed, I remember him very well," said Sarah slowly as she held the door open for her mistress.

Anne patted her cheek on parting. "So you will come with me to my new home, be my comfort, and make life tolerable," she said with a smile.

So at least there is one matter upon which they are agreed reflected Sarah bitterly as she quietly closed the door and set about tidying the room. When she had finished she sank down by the window and gazed forlornly out. As if in tune with her mood the sky had clouded over, the lovely day had gone. It would rain tomorrow.

She sat there for a long time, watching the shadows stealthily creeping across the little park, like a cloaked and hooded army silently closing in on the house. There was a new moon which appeared shyly and only occasionally when there was a break in the cloud. Sarah supposed she should wish—curtsy—turn silver in her pocket but she had no silver and as for a wish, what hope of it coming true. Her fate, too, was apparently decided for her. To be a servant and companion a looker-on, for the rest of her life. Resolutely she tried not to think about the wild dream she had entertained less than an hour ago as she raced back to the house before returning to her duties.

Sarah was without guile, although she was already nineteen. Men had played no part in her life. She had had neither the time nor inclination to dally with the serving men at High Hall, which was the only world she knew. Her position in the household as confidante and companion to the daughters of the house together with her own inate dignity and reserve had protected her from the lusty rough and tumble of the servants hall. Even Mistress Fitch expected her to be treated as a waiting gentlewoman. This was not from any particular fondness for Sarah but for the simple reason that the newly landed Fitchs could not afford nor did they indeed possess a suitable young relative of their own to fill this position, as was usual in a nobleman's house. Sarah made an excellent substitute, satisfying Mistress Fitch's pride without her feeling obliged to find her a husband and provide a dowry. Sarah's position, therefore, was somewhat invidious and she did not entirely escape the amorous attentions of some new and over enthusiastic footman. Such overtures she ignored with cool disdain, when another maid would loudly protest or giggle, and her calm disregard of such clumsy importunities soon forbade anything further. Henry Berkeley, however, had from their first meeting aroused in her quite different feelings. She had found him friendly and attractive and although she had at that time repelled his advances knowing that he was pledged to her mistress, she had secretly and lightheartedly enjoyed his pursuit which had never been unpleasant and had become a sort of game between them. Alone now in the darkening room, she blushed hotly with shame and anger when she thought of the fairytale future she had imagined for herself after their meeting that afternoon. Believing him to be no longer a suitor for Anne, supplanted as she thought by another of more consequence; captured again by his charm, remembering his past attentions and not entirely unaware of her own beauty, she had dared to believe it possible that it was for herself he had returned to High Hall.

"Fool! fool! fool!" she murmured bitterly to the remote uninterested stars. But nothing could now alter the fact that she had that day lost her heart and Sarah was not of those who could retrieve it hastily and await the time to dispose of it more sensibly.

5 Henry William Berkeley Portman returns with a marriage licence

HENRY SEYMOUR PORTMAN died in 1727 at the age of eighty-eight. His young wife Meliora was very soon married again to a local fox-hunting Squire, Thomas Fownes of Stepleton, and the estates Henry had inherited from his cousin, Sir William Portman, passed to his kinsman, William Berkeley of Pylle, who finally took the name and arms of Portman by Act of Parliament in 1736.

William was a member of a younger branch of the Berkeleys of Berkeley Castle, Gloucestershire. To find the source of his Portman blood it was necessary for William to trace his ancestry back over a hundred years to Sir John Portman the first Baronet, for the Berkeleys of Pylle were descended from Sir John's youngest daughter, Joan, to whose heirs Sir William had devised his estates by further provisions of his will, in the event of Henry dying childless. Joan's daughter, Phillipa, had married Edward Berkeley. William was their only surviving grandson.

Although the Portman connection was remote and the blood well diluted by this time, it nevertheless flowed more strongly in the veins of William Berkeley's children for he had married Anne Seymour, a daughter of Sir Edward, Henry's eldest brother, who also traced her descent through her grandmother from Sir John.

If Sir William Portman's spirit sometimes rode a ghostly steed over the Dorset hills and down to his beloved valley, he must have been well pleased. For even with all his careful planning he could not have foreseen that the grandchildren of both his aunts by uniting Seymours and Berkeleys in marriage would fortify and strengthen the Portman line which he was so anxious should survive.

William Berkeley could not, however, have found it very easy to relinquish his own name. The Berkeleys were a proud and ancient family who traced their descent from Robert, Duke of Normandy, father of the Conqueror, and to Roger de Berkeley, a Saxon nobleman related to Edward the Confessor. They were noble before the Conquest—when the Portmans were unknown Squires in Somerset. William, however, was fortunate in having two sons, so there was no reason why one of them should not retain the Berkeley name. Perhaps it was their father's reluctance to surrender his own birthright which delayed for so long, nearly ten years, the Act of Parliament which enabled him to take the name and bear the Arms of Portman. In the meanwhile, however, he entered into and enjoyed his inheritance. In the map showing the destruction done by the fire of Blandford, in 1731, Bryanston—on the bend of the river just out of the town—is shown as the residence of William Portman, Esq. He was also one of the trustees of the public funds raised for the relief and restoration of the town. During that ten years he resided alternately between his three seats—Orchard Portman, Bryanston and his own manor of Pylle, where he died and was buried in 1737. By his will, his eldest son, Edward, kept the family name and estates, whilst Henry William, the younger, inherited the far more valuable Portman estates. The material benefits were evidently considered to be of less importance to the Berkeleys than the continuation by the eldest son of the Berkeley name.

Henry could have had no quarrel with this point of view, for like Henry Seymour before him, being a younger son, it was no hardship to make this sacrifice in exchange for the rich and unexpected gift of the fine estates in the West Country. Tradition is a poor substitute for meat and the younger sons of great families, brought up on a rich diet, very often go hungry in later life.

Henry Berkeley was twenty-eight when his father died. He had spent most of his adult life in the Metropolis where he had been busy sowing his wild oats in the approved manner, enjoying life enormously and accumulating a great many debts. Although gambling accounted for much of them, he could no more resist a pretty face than he could a wager. Both these expensive weaknesses were common to most of his friends. In addition, however, he suffered from a complete inability to refuse financial help to anyone from a Lord to a pot-boy who asked it of him. He was delighted with his estates which he found in excellent order. Henry Seymour, who had enjoyed them for forty years, had spared no expense in making improvements. He had laid out the most elaborate gardens at both Orchard Portman and at Bryanston where his riverside plantations were already becoming famous. So proud was old Henry of his achievements that he had commissioned Knyff to record the layout of both manors. This the artist did in his curious architectural style, with entire disregard of perspective, and meticulous inclusion of every out-building, tree, path, gate and shrub. Even an aerial photograph could not have produced a clearer picture for posterity.

Henry Berkeley was determined to become a worthy successor. He would settle down to the life of a country Squire, be a good landlord, eschewing the pleasures of the town, except for occasional relaxation. He would marry Anne Fitch, chosen for him long since by his father, endeavour to be a good husband and remain at least as faithful to her as the fashion of the times expected.

The choice of Anne Fitch was not without reason. In a day when inter-marriage between local landed families was inevitable it was important to introduce new blood from time to time, a biological necessity of which the English gentleman has always been well aware. The Fitch's were newcomers to Dorset. John Fitch, the founder of the family fortunes was a London builder and architect, who had achieved some eminence and wealth in the rebuilding of the City after the Great Fire. Amongst other public works, his contract with the Lord Mayor and Governors of the City to enlarge, deepen, and cleanse the Fleet ditch, which until this time was nothing but an open sewer and breeder of lethal germs, not only proved of immense benefit to the population of the City but also considerably enlarged his fortune.

His son William, a scholar and a gentleman of polished manners, bought High Hall, near Wimborne in Dorset, and became one of the newly landed gentry on the proceeds. He raised a large family of three sons and four daughters; thereby introducing healthy new blood into the county. It was no coincidence that both Henry Seymour and his young kinsman after him should seek their brides from the sisters at High Hall in a considered attempt to fulfill their trust and revive the Portman family. If the choice of a wife was not his own, Henry was happy to abide by his late father's wishes and saw no reason to disregard them now that he was his own master. Anne was beautiful and if a little cold he was confident he would soon remedy that. He knew her to be accomplished in all the domestic arts and was sure she would make a perfect chatelaine. If her breeding was not of the highest he was assured that her upbringing could leave nothing to be desired. It had undoubtedly been far more careful and painstaking than was customary in families of higher birth who did not feel the same necessity to impress. Henry's only regret was that he had not sacrificed one year of bachelorhood, and pleased his father by marrying in his lifetime. Now he determined to lose no more time. As soon as his father was buried in the family vault at Pylle, he left immediately for Bryanston, taking with him his sister Laetitia.

The eighteen year old Laetitia was to supervise the household until the arrival of his bride, whom he intended to marry forthwith, her parents' consent having been obtained on his visit to them nearly a year ago. It did not occur to Henry as at all odd that after this long absence, during which time he had made no attempt to communicate with or see his future wife, he should now demand that they be married just as soon as all legal arrangements were completed.

His letter to High Hall announcing his intention preceeded his own arrival by no more than a few days, and he did not mean to leave until the marriage was solemnised and he could take his bride back with him to Bryanston.

He left his sister to supervise the final preparations for Anne's reception with some misgivings, for he considered her to be an example of the well-bred girl badly brought up. Laetitia was the only daughter and many years younger than both her brothers and although agreeing well enough with Edward, she tormented Henry who had so far found her the only woman he was unable to handle.

It was not surprising that Mr. Berkeley Portman's arrival at High Hall, armed with a special licence from the Bishop, should have thrown the house into a ferment. A ferment of hasty preparations for the wedding; of joy on the part of an ambitious mother and of despair on the part of the unwilling bride, given no choice and no time to contrive her escape. But the worst ferment of all was in the heart of young Sarah Godwyn. Her misery was unshared and indeed unknown to anyone but herself as with outward calm she sorted and packed her Mistress's belongings and assembled her own few possessions for the short bridal journey to Bryanston.

**Bryanston House, with the arms of the Rogers family, about 1658.
This oil painting was found in the Berni Inn, Taunton,
which in the fifteenth century was the Portman town house.**

Bryanston House, engraved by Johannes Kip in his work on 'The principal seats of the Nobility and Gentry of Great Britain', 1708.

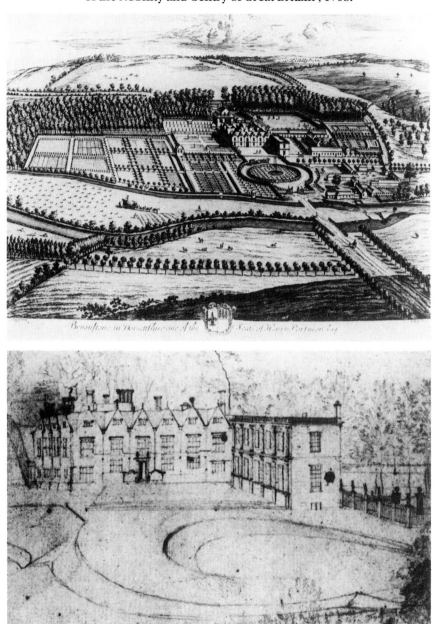

Bryanston House, sketched by Thomas Robins, about 1750.

**Sir William Portman[1644-89], the last baronet, who captured the
Duke of Monmouth in 1685.
He bought the Bryanston estate about 1660.**

Thomas Gainsborough's painting of Henry William Berkeley Portman. [Died 1761.]

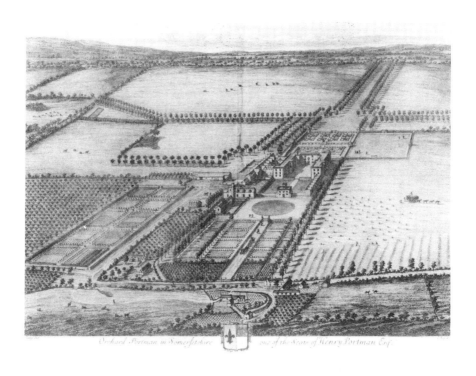

Orchard Portman in Somersetshire   one of the Seats of Henry Portman Esq.

Orchard Portman House, near Taunton, engraved by Johannes Kip for his 1708 work.

The Berkeley family tree, from John Hutchins's County History.

Pedigree of BERKELEY PORTMAN, showing the descent from Robert Duke of Normandy, the Fitzhardings, Berkeleys, &c. &c.

Berkeley Castle, Gloucestershire.

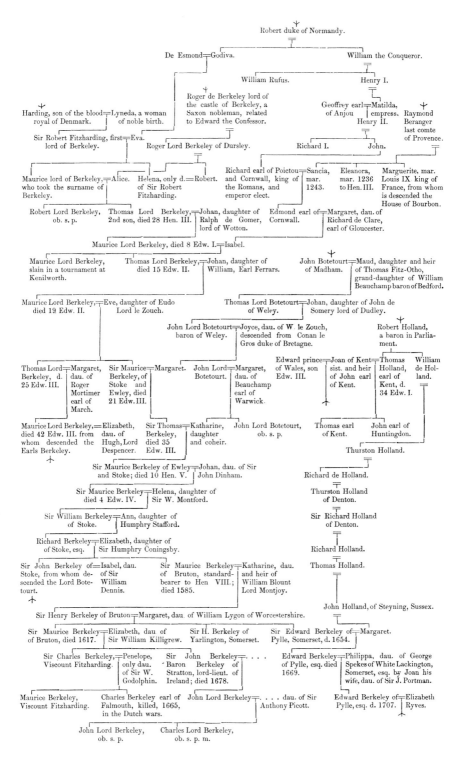

Pedigree of BERKELEY PORTMAN of Bryanston.

Arms: 1, 4, Or, a fleur-de-lys az.; 2, 3, gules, a chevron ermine between ten crosslets pattée arg.

Crests: A talbot sejant or. A unicorn passant gules gorged with a ducal coronet and chain or.

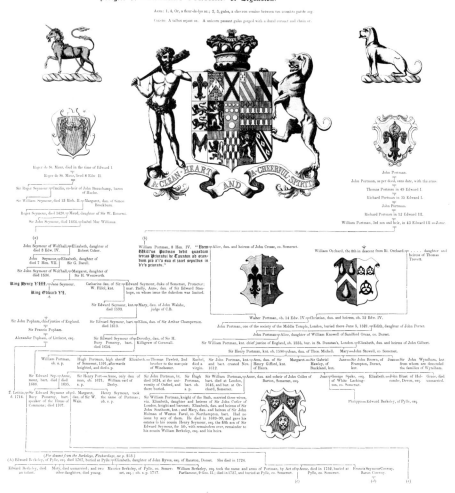

Roger de St. Maur, died in the time of Edward I.

Roger de St. Maur, lived 8 Edw. II.

Sir Roger Seymour=Cecilia, co-heir of John Beauchamp, baron of Hache.

Sir William Seymour, died 13 Rich. II.=Margaret, dau. of Simon Brockburn.

Roger Seymour, died 1420.=Maud, daughter of Sir W. Esturmi.

Sir John Seymour, died 1464.=Isabel Mac Williams.

John Portman.

John Portman, as per deed, sans date, with the arms.

Thomas Portman in 49 Edward I.

Richard Portman in 35 Edward I.

John Portman.

Richard Portman in 12 Edward III.

William Portman, 3rd son and heir, in 43 Edward III =Joane.

(a)
John Seymour of Wolfhall,=Elizabeth, daughter of died 3 Edw. IV. Robert Coker.

John Seymour,=Elizabeth, daughter of died 7 Hen. VII. Sir G. Darell.

Sir John Seymour of Wolfhall,=Margaret, daughter of died 1536. Sir H. Wentworth.

King Henry VIII.=Jane Seymour.

King Edward VI.

Sir John Popham, chief justice of England.

Sir Francis Popham.

Alexander Popham, of Littlecot, esq.

(b)
William Portman, 8 Hen. IV. "Item=Alice, dau. and heiress of John Crosse, co. Somerset. Will'us Portman debt quasdam terras Prioratui de Taunton ab oratu-bum pro a'i'a sua et iacet sepultus in b'c'o prioratu."

Catharine dau. of Sir=Edward Seymour, duke of Somerset, Protector; W. Filiol, knt. mar. 2ndly, Anne, dau. of Sir Edward Stanhope, on whose issue the dukedom was limited.

Sir Edward Seymour, knt.=Mary, dau. of John Walshe, died 1593. judge of C.B.

Sir Edward Seymour, bart.=Eliza, dau. of Sir Arthur Champernon. died 1613.

Sir Edward Seymour=Dorothy, dau. of Sir H. Bury Pomeroy, Killigrew of Cornwall. bart. died 1654.

William Orchard, the 8th in descent from Ri. Orchard.=. . . . daughter and heiress of Thomas Trevett.

Walter Portman, ob. 14 Edw. IV.=Christian, dau. and heiress, ob. 12 Edw. IV.

John Portman, one of the society of the Middle Temple, London, buried there June 5, 1521.=Edith, daughter of John Porter.

John Portman=Alice, daughter of William Knowell of Sandford Orcas, co. Dorset.

Sir William Portman, knt. chief justice of England, ob. 1555, bur. in St. Dunstan's, London.=Elizabeth, dau. and heiress of John Gilbert.

Sir Henry Portman, knt. ob. 1590=Joan, dau. of Thos. Mitchell. Mary=John Stowell, co. Somerset.

| William Portman, ob. s. p. | Hugh Portman, high sheriff of Somerset, 1591, afterwards knighted, and died s. p. | Elizabeth=Thomas Pawlett, 2nd brother to the marquis of Winchester. | Rachel, died a virgin. | Sir John Portman, knt.=Ann, dau. of Sir and bart. created Nov. Henry Gifford, knt. 1612. of Hants. | Margaret=Sir Gabriel Hawley, of Buckland, knt. | June=Sir John Brown, of Frampton, Dorset. | Joan=Sir John Wyndham, knt. from whom are descended the families of Wyndham. |

Sir Edward Sey-=Anne, mour, bart. died only dau of 1688. man, ob. 1621, William earl of Derby.

Sir Henry Port=Anne, only dau of William earl of Derby.

Sir John Portman, bart. at the university of Oxford, and there buried.

Sir Hugh Portman, bart. ob. 1646, and bur. at Orchard, Somerset.

Sir William Portman,=Anne, dau. and coheir of John Colles of bart. died at London, Barton, Somerset, esq. 1646, and bur. at Orchard, Somerset.

Joan=George Speke, esq. of White Lacking-ton, co. Somerset.

Elizabeth=John Bluet of Hol-combe, Devon, esq.

Grace, died unmarried.

?. Letitia,=Sir Edward Seymour of=1. Margaret, d. 1714. Bury Pomeroy, dau. of Sir W. speaker of the House of Wale. Commons; died 1707.

2. Henry Seymour, took the name of Portman; ob. s. p.

Sir William Portman, knight of the Bath, married three wives, viz. Elizabeth, daughter and heiress of Sir John Cutler of London, knight and baronet; Elizabeth, dau. and heiress of Sir John Southcott, knt.; and Mary, dau. and heiress of Sir John Holman of Weston Favel, co. Northampton, bart. Had no issue by any of them. He died in 1689-90, and gave his estates to his cousin Henry Seymour, esq. the fifth son of Sir Edward Seymour, for life, with remainders over, remainder to his cousin William Berkeley, esq. and his heirs.

Philippa=Edward Berkeley, of Pylle, esq.

(For descent from the Berkeleys, Fitzhardinge, see p. 253.)

(A) Edward Berkeley, of Pylle, esq. died 1707, buried at Pylle.=Elizabeth, daughter of John Ryves, esq. of Ranston, Dorset. She died in 1724.

Edward Berkeley, died Mary, died unmarried; and two Maurice Berkeley, of Pylle, co. Somer- William Berkeley, esq. took the name and arms of Portman, by Act of=Anne, died in 1752, buried at Francis Seymour Conway. an infant. other daughters, died young. set, esq.; ob. s. p. 1717. Parliament, 9 Geo. II.; died 1787, and buried at Pylle, co. Somerset. Pylle, co. Somerset. Baron Conway.

(b) (c) (d) (e)

The Berkeley Portman family tree, from John Hutchins's County History.

Edward Berkeley Portman MP, father of the first Viscount Portman. [1771-1823.]

Mrs Elizabeth Montagu [1720-1800], **the leading hostess in London society and the instigator of 'blue-stocking' conversation parties. She built Montagu House** [later Portman House] **in the north-west corner of Portman Square, Marylebone, in 1781.**

Montagu House [22 Portman Square] **was designed for Elizabeth Montagu by James Stuart. It was destroyed by German bombing in the Second World War.**
[The Portman Hotel now occupies its site.]

The north side of Portman Square – the first development on the London estate.

22 Portman Square: the hall.

22 Portman Square: the saloon.

**Streets begin to fill the Portman Estate in the parish of St Mary le Bone.
The map is by James Horwood, 1794.**

Home House, Portman Square – one of the finest Adams houses in London.
Robert and James Adams introduced elegant curves and other refinements to
soften the rigid classical lines of Georgian architecture.

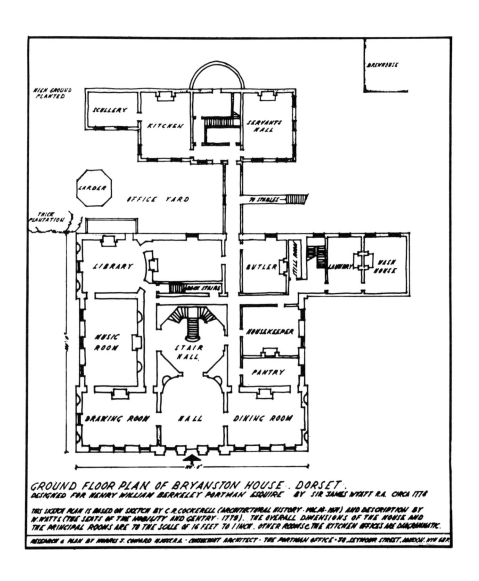

Ground floor plan of Bryanston House, Dorset, designed by Sir James Wyatt in 1778. [Research: Morris J. Coward.]

6   The two ladies
arrive at Bryanston

HENRY AND ANNE were married within a week of the bridegroom's arrival at High Hall. To Mistress Fitch's eternal regret her desire for the maximum fuss and frills and the opportunity to impress her neighbours and enhance her own importance was lost forever. The shortness of time cheated her not only of an elaborate, ostentatious ceremony but also of weeks of delicious pre-wedding gossip of past weddings, of brides, dowries and fortunes; of bridegrooms, scoundrels, rakes or perfect gentlemen; of babies unborn or born too soon. Amidst the tinkle of the tea cups, ladylike shrieks of laughter and venom whispered behind fans, who is most deferred to, who the greatest authority on these matters but the mother of a new bride-to-be. She, the heroine of every female gathering, preening herself and basking in the congratulations, masked envy and admiration of her masterly handling of her darling puppet, whose silken strings she will soon hand over to an eminently eligible bridegroom.

Mistress Fitch would have revelled in it all, it was quite cruel that these delights should all have to be crammed into one short week. The solemn vows of two young people, to her, were of considerably less importance. Anne, however, was a lovely bride in her simple white gown and Henry, dark-haired, broad-shouldered, with his full share of Berkeley good looks made a perfect foil for her fragile, pale gold beauty. The ceremony in the Minster at Wimborne did not appear to lack anything of importance.

The wedding celebrations were to last but one day for Mr. Portman had early announced his intention to leave for Bryanston by noon the next morning. Unable to dissuade him Mistress Fitch had to make the best of this and the wedding breakfast was as lavish as she could make it and enjoyed by more guests than could be comfortably crammed into High Hall. Not that anyone minded this in the least so long as the wine flowed and the festivities continued well into the night. Henry enjoyed his wedding day as he enjoyed most things. He too drank his fill with Anne's brothers but not so much that he was unable to defeat their intention of seeing the bride and bridegroom bedded in the old-fashioned manner. Anne had retired early but by the time her brothers decided to set about their self-imposed task of escorting Henry to her chamber, the bridegroom was apparently fast asleep in his chair with his head pillowed on the dining table. Their attempts to arouse him received no response, but their boisterous efforts to lift him bodily were so violently and ill-received that they very shortly gave up the whole idea and left him to sleep undisturbed. They were never to know that the door had scarcely closed behind them, when the "intoxicated" bridegroom raised his head and with a grin reached for a decanter. Having given them time to disperse to their own apartments, he made his way quietly to his wife's room only to find the door securely locked and no response to his gentle tap. With a good humoured shrug he returned to the dining parlour where, having finished the wine on the table he settled down to spend his wedding night alone, with the untidy remains of the marriage feast scattered around him.

Soon after three o'clock in the afternoon of the next day, Mr. Portman's travelling coach clattered over the cobblestones of Blandford Market Place. It attracted a great deal of attention from the townsfolk for it was not often that they had the pleasure of seeing such an elegant equippage, drawn by four brown horses of impeccable breeding and good looks, and the interest was increased by the rumour that the young Squire's bride was its occupant. Henry, in spite of infrequent appearances at Bryanston, was already well-liked in the neighbourhood, both as his father's son and on his own account. His father had done a great deal for the distressed and homeless townspeople after the disasterous fire which had not only almost totally destroyed Blandford, but also the two neighbouring villages, across the river, of Blandford St. Mary and Bryanston, the latter his own property. Fortunately, the manor house itself and the church, a mile distant up the river, were unaffected by the conflagration.

The disaster and his subsequent help and interest in the plight both of his own tenants and the townsfolk had gained an entree for himself and his family, which under normal circumstances he would have waited many years to achieve. Dorset folk were proverbially suspicious of "foreigners", even when they came from neighbouring Somerset. The son they had soon found to be an open-handed young gentleman, with a friendly charm which endeared him to people in all walks of life. His entrance into the town after his marriage, riding beside the coach, was greeted warmly with smiles and salutes from everyone on the busy streets. Whilst acknowledging these, Henry found time to point out to the coach's passengers the fine brick-built houses, the Town Hall and the church, all new built, of which the town was justly proud, for in the words of J. Bastard, the Architect chiefly responsible, Blandford "had arisen like a Phoenix from the ashes", and was undoubtedly a great improvement on the insanitary old huddle of wood and thatch which had succumbed so quickly to the fire and its ally, a relentless north wind.

The progress of the coach with its outrider through the busy market square was necessarily slow, and when they reached the Greyhound Inn the procession came to a halt whilst pleasantries were exchanged with the Landlord waiting outside his fine new hostelry. Here Henry checked his timepiece and informed his bride with great delight that the journey from Wimborne had taken less than two hours and boasted that, had the road been better, his horses could have done it in half the time. Anne smiled politely, but as soon as Henry's head was removed from the window she turned to Sarah and remarked with a sigh: "We should indeed then be grateful for the bad state of the roads, for I swear if we had travelled at a greater pace we would have overturned and spilled out on the road like a basket of eggs—with equally disasterous results I do not doubt."

Sarah scarcely heeded her, she had eyes and ears only for the sights and sounds outside the coach, as she had had throughout the journey. Never having travelled further than Wimborne in her life, everything was new and exciting, and in spite of her heart-ache she had enjoyed every minute of the journey. She had made a half-hearted attempt before the wedding to persuade Anne to leave her at High Hall but it was too difficult without being able to give any real reason, and when Anne insisted that she accompany her, Sarah gave in, knowing in her heart that the pain of living in the same house as Henry and his new bride could not be worse than the agony of never seeing him again. Nevertheless she found it necessary to assure herself constantly that she had done everything possible in her dependant position to avoid going with them; that Henry, newly married, would pay no further attention to her; and that if by chance he should, her own principles and moral convictions would protect her. The small voice of conscience which persisted in reminding her of the danger that lay in her love for Henry, coupled with the fact that Anne did not care for him anyway, she ignored, though the thought remained uneasily in her subconscious mind.

Henry signalled to his coachman to move on and amid the good wishes of mine host and his servants, and the friendly waves and curtseys of the onlookers, the great coach moved slowly on up the hill.

In a few minutes they had left the town behind them and were on the treelined road which led down across the meadows to the bridge which carried them over the river and straight on to the great circular driveway leading to the forecourt of the old Manor House of Bryanston. Here was all bustle and excitement—a host of servants and retainers awaited them and as Henry quickly leapt from his horse and opened the door of the coach to help his bride descend, a great cheer went up. Anne acknowledged it with her usual gentle grace. Henry, proud and happy, with one arm about her, did not forget Sarah. With his eyes on his bride, he held out his hand to steady the maid as she descended the step, but so absorbed was he in the reception for Anne that somehow he forgot to release the girl's hand immediately and for a brief moment the three of them stood together. It was as if Henry had brought back two brides to Bryanston. Gently Sarah disengaged her hand from Henry's warm clasp and stepped back a pace as the Steward and the Housekeeper came forward to greet their new mistress.

She watched as Henry swept Anne into his arms and carried her over the threshold of his house.

The coach clattered off towards the stables followed by grooms and stable boys. Everyone else crowded through the great oak door in the wake of the bride and groom. Before she followed Sarah stole a moment to look about her and enjoy a wider view than she had had from the window of the coach. The house was situated on rising ground on a little plateau between the river and the cliff which rose steeply behind it. Below, the calm waters of the Stour swept in a wide graceful curve towards her, where they divided into two streams, leaving between them a narrow green island on which a few cattle grazed in an isolated world of their own, linked to either bank only by the two slender arched bridges. Beyond the twin streams, the tree studded parkland clothed in the golden green of early summer rose gently towards the hills.

"Mr. Berkeley" had not exaggerated the beautiful situation of his "neighbour's" house she reflected, wondering if his description of its domestic inconveniences were equally accurate. She turned to look up at the great gabled house, snuggled close into the hillside. Its weathered stone, grey-green like the trunk of a beech tree, splashed with gold in the sunlight and shadowed with the shifting black lace patterns of nearby trees looked as though it too had grown out of the ground itself. Well she would very soon find out for herself she decided as she hastened to join the household gathered inside.

If Sarah had delayed a few moments longer she would have been rewarded by the sight of two riders cantering over the bridge. The leader, some distance ahead of the other, was a girl and she appeared to be in haste for she did not spare the horse up the little rise or draw rein until she reached the forecourt. Yelling something to the following groom she dismounted without assistance and tossing the long skirts of her green velvet habit over her arm abandoned the horse and hurried towards the house. Most of the household had already been presented to their new mistress by the time the horsewoman reached the great hall where they were all assembled. Sarah, who had found her way there after some difficulty, having lost herself in the inner courtyard, was the first to notice the young woman's entrance. She swept in, prodded two broad backs which blocked her passage with her riding whip and swiftly made her way through the ranks towards the bride and groom. Sarah watched with interest as the girl approached, admiring the elegance of the velvet habit and the plumed hat beneath which was a haughty little face and enormous eyes fixed with cool appraisal on Anne.

As she reached them Henry turned to her, "Well, ma'am, how kind. So you have condescended to arrive at last to welcome my wife to Bryanston." He bowed low. "I do sincerely hope we have not put you to any inconvenience."

"No indeed, of that you can rest assured. However I did not expect you so soon" she replied, "Now since I am here, perhaps you will kindly present your wife to me."

"No, my autocratic infant, but I will gladly present *you* to my wife." He took his wife's hand, "Anne, I wish to present my sister, Laetitia, who should have been here to greet us, but was unavoidably detained", he paused, and slowly let his gaze travel over the girl from plumed hat to sweeping hem, "by a new mare and a fine afternoon" he added dryly.

The two ladies curtseyed. Anne gave Henry a puzzled look, but Laetitia unmoved, did not take her eyes from Anne's face. Then she leant forward and lightly kissed her cheek.

"Why," she cried, "I am delighted with my new sister. How pretty you are, I did not expect it. Now tell me, why have you not married before this? You must surely have had many offers all these years."

Anne murmured inaudibly. A reply to this was impossible and

fortunately unnecessary for Laetitia ran on gaily, apparently
unaware of any lack of tact in her remarks which continued to be
insufferably patronizing and outrageous, delivered with the wide-
eyed enthusiasm of a child anxious to please.

Henry's face was thunderous. As soon as possible he summoned
the housekeeper to take Anne to her own apartments, firmly telling
Laetitia that it was not in the least necessary for her to accompany
them.

7   Henry's turbulent sister

"THE LADY LAETITIA is a bitch," said Sarah, rummaging in her mistress's deepest chest to find the most elegant gown the bride possessed.

Anne looked at her in surprise—

"Why, 'tis not like you, Sarah, to speak so.   She is but a child, and talks carelessly without regard . . ."

"Aye, and will always remain a child," Sarah interrupted crossly, "and always will speak as she pleases.   With those great innocent eyes to protect her from a charge of malice."

"Fiddle, child," Anne shrugged.   Never having had any wish to compete with her own sex, Laetitia's remarks at their first meeting had surprised, but not in the least offended or hurt her.   "We dine fashionably late, I understand," she went on, "I think I will rest for an hour for I swear every bone in my body is aching after that tiresome journey.   You go and seek your own chamber Sarah.   I pray it is not too far away, or we may never find each other again in this warren."   She sighed, "How different it is from my father's neat house."

Sarah, who did not share her mistress's view, was only too glad to be released and to have an opportunity to explore more of their new home, which, if rambling and old-fashioned compared to High Hall, built as recently as the late Queen Anne's reign, was nevertheless all the more interesting and exciting for that very reason.

She first helped her mistress out of her travelling gown, loosened the numerous strings of petticoats and stays, and begging Anne to try to sleep a little she left her comfortably disposed on the great four-poster bed, promising to return within the hour.

When she had gone Anne closed her eyes and tried to follow Sarah's advice.   She was tired enough, but tense with nervous dread of her next ordeal, dining alone for the first time with this stranger who was her husband.   No, not quite alone, Laetitia would undoubtedly be present.   She wondered if this would make it any easier.   Certainly her first encounter with her young sister-in-law had not been exactly encouraging.   Finally, from sheer exhaustion, she slept and did not wake until Sarah returned to help her dress. She was just about ready when there was a scratch at the door and Henry himself appeared to escort his wife down to dinner.   He expressed his pleasure at her appearance and admired her gown and coiffeur over which Sarah had taken unusual pains determined that in looks at least her mistress should compete on equal terms with her sister-in-law. Anne took Henry's proferred arm and through shadowy corridors, where the only light was the red glow of the evening sun struggling to penetrate one or two distant windows, he led her downstairs to the small dining room, where Laetitia this time awaited them. Anne took her place opposite Henry at the long table, bright with the soft light of many candles.

Laetitia, seated between them, was silent at first and looked sulky, quite different from the exuberant child who had greeted her. Anne wondered if Henry had rebuked her for her absence on their arrival. However, that she decided was no concern of hers and as she sipped her wine, she began to relax. Glad of the presence of a third person at the table she erroneously supposed that her first evening at Bryanston would not be the ordeal she had imagined.

Perhaps if Anne had had the advantage of a better acquaintance with her husband, or even had been less nervous and taken more part in the conversation, it might have been less stormy. As it was, after the first meaningless polite exchanges between three people with no mutual interests, one of whom was virtually a stranger, it was eventually left entirely to familiarities between brother and sister. Starting with thinly veiled polite sarcasm on both sides, it worked up to blatantly acrimonious remarks from each in turn. Finally with no-one to mediate it blew up into a full scale family row of the kind that had been usual between brother and sister since Laetitia was old enough to string a sentence together, with insults flying backwards and forwards across the table like buns at a boisterous childrens tea party. To do him justice, Henry was not the instigator. Laetitia could flaunt her feminine charm like a banner, fluttering long eyelashes indiscriminately at footmen, curates and her brother's friends. Or wield it as a sword to prick and wound according to her mood. Yet she rebelled furiously at the restrictions of her sex and deeply regretted she was not a boy. Her brother, of whose independence she was wildly jealous, was the natural victim on whom she could vent her frustrations and punish for this oversight on nature's part. He, however, was a match for her. Although not easily roused, his temper was as hot as her own and when his sister chose to discard the gentle manners expected of her sex and enter the arena sacred to the male, he was fully prepared to do battle.

Anne watched and listened in complete bewilderment. Whatever qualms she had had about her first day at Bryanston, she had certainly not expected this. There was no longer any need or indeed opportunity for her to utter the polite inanities which she had forced from herself earlier. In fact they both seemed to have completely forgotten her presence until a remark of Laetitia's about his marriage drew Henry's attention to his bride.

With a wave of his hand as if dismissing Laetitia and her importunities he turned to Anne.

"You find your new home agreeable I trust, ma'am, and your apartments I hope?"

"Indeed yes. I thank you sir," Anne replied softly.

"There are many improvements to be made," Henry went on. "My father lived mostly at Pylle, but I intend to reside mainly here at Bryanston. It is a charming estate and an easy ride on fair roads to London."

"That is, of course, of the first importance," Laetitia interrupted, "important business will take your husband to town all too often."

Henry ignored her.

"The coverts here are excellent," he went on, "better far than at Orchard in Somerset, and you are aware, I suppose, that your brother-in-law, Mr. Fownes of Stepleton, is a close neighbour and keeps a pack of fox-hounds which are said to be some of the best in the whole country."

"How interesting your sweet Anne must find this information, since she neither shoots nor hunts, though no doubt she may look forward to ministering to your comforts when you return from these pursuits." Laetitia refused to be silenced. Her childish spite was unsuppressible.

Henry turned to her once more. "You, dear sister, would be cold comfort to any man. By God, I'd as soon bed with a rattle-snake as take you to wife."

They were away again, once more the verbal battle raged across the candle-lit table. Anne, confused and miserable, wished only to escape. In her own home she had witnessed nothing more than girlish squabbles and tantrums, and not one of her sisters would have dared to speak to their elder brothers as Laetitia did to Henry. The naked rage and bitter feeling which flared in a second between these two was something she could not understand.

"Your attitude is offensive and does you no credit, and your insults do not concern me at all," Laetitia's voice shook with an anger which belied her words. "It would perhaps be to your advantage to put on a better face before your bride at this early stage. Though indeed I doubt not but you would find it difficult to maintain."

With a slightly trembling hand she toyed with a heavy silver fork and went on. "Heigh ho. Perhaps 'tis as well. Poor wretch, she will find out all too soon that with your drinking and your wenching it will be no sinecure to be Mistress of Bryanston. I wish her joy of it," she added spitefully.

There was a roar from Henry, which seemed to echo and bounce from wall to wall of the panelled room, and his reply was so offensive that it must have even shaken the impassivity of the menservants standing silently in the shadows. As for Laetitia, it left her speechless but not out of action.

Anne looked at her nervously. The fork was still in the girl's hand and Anne gasped involuntarily as she raised it. Surely she would not? More speculation was unnecessary. There was the sharp crack of metal against glass. Anne, her eyes following the red stream of spilled wine snake silently across the table towards her, was at the same time aware of something bright and shining flying through the air. Narrowly missing Henry's head the fork landed with a crash at the feet of the immobile footman who stood some paces behind his master. As the man, after a moment's hesitation, bent down to retrieve it, Anne burst into tears and fled from the room.

8   *First night blues*

SARAH SOFTLY closed the door of her mistress's bedroom, straightened her shoulders and took a deep breath before setting off down the corridor.   She was quite certain that the message she had to carry to Mr. Portman would not be well received and wondered with some trepidation just what his reaction would be.   To have to convey this particular message to a man on what was virtually his wedding night was not the most enviable task in any circumstances, and Sarah had begged her mistress to reconsider or at least find someone else to approach him.   To no avail.   Anne was completely upset by the incident at dinner.   Resignation had fled and misery and revulsion had returned in full force.   Nothing Sarah could say would persuade her that Henry William was not the monster of her imagination.   As for a different messenger who but Sarah could she send in this house of strangers.

As she slipped quietly down the unfamiliar stairs, her candle held high, Sarah discovered that her heart was thumping in the most alarming manner.   She had exchanged no more than a few words with Henry, and then always in the company of others, since the afternoon of his arrival at High Hall.   It was therefore as much on her own account that she dreaded the interview with him to which she was now committed.   She did not doubt that she would find him alone in the dining parlour, and in all probability now slightly drunk.

In this she was correct.   As she entered she found he was sitting facing her at the head of the table on which the candles were burning low.   Elsewhere they had all been extinguished so that the rest of the room was dark.   Sarah advanced only a few steps, hoping to remain anonymous in the shadows, deliver her message and depart immediately.   However she was not to escape so easily.

"Why damme, its the nymph of the beechwood," Henry drawled, "come in, come in.   I feared you had turned into a mouse this past week.   All I ever see is a little grey back scuttling away from me."

Sarah gave a bob and wished him good evening.   Mouse indeed! Her nervousness left her through sheer indignation.

"I bring a message from my Mistress," she said in a firm voice, then hesitated.

"Indeed, pray continue," Henry prompted her.

"She is fatigued Sir, after the journey," Sarah went on with less confidence. "She is a little distraught, unwell . . . and, and . . . begs that you excuse her and will kindly leave her undisturbed this night," she finished with a rush.

Henry's face hardened, for a moment he said nothing, then reaching for a candlestick from the table he held it high and rose a little unsteadily to his feet. His voice was cold and quite different from his usual good-humoured drawl as he advanced towards her.

"Then let us take a closer look at the charming messenger. Possibly my wife supposed I would accept a substitute."

Sarah stood quite still as he tilted up her chin and stared down into her eyes, but her heart was in a turmoil. Every instinct in her body longed for him to put his arms around her and take the kisses he had sought so light-heartedly at their first meetings. With the least encouragement on her part she knew he would do so. But it was not moral scruples alone which prevented her giving it, the greater deterrent was her own pride allied to the knowledge that hurt and angry as he was with Anne, she herself meant no more to him than a pretty girl with whom he would be pleased to amuse himself and seek temporary consolation for his wife's indifference and distaste.

"My wife is most considerate," Henry was saying, "I could not myself have improved upon her choice. Our charming, elusive Sarah," he shook his head and released her.

She hesitated for a moment as he turned away and carefully replaced the candlestick on the table, and watched as he slowly poured himself a glass of wine, then murmuring goodnight, Sarah made to leave.

"Wait," Henry's voice was soft, no longer angry. He filled a second glass. "Come, drink a toast with me Sarah," he picked up the two glasses and handed one to her. Raising his own high, he gave the toast.

"To my sons," he said. Sarah sipped obediently while Henry emptied his glass. "It is my intention to have at least two sons. To achieve this object," he went on dryly, "it is necessary that I sleep with my wife, that is if they are to be legitimate. Inform my Lady that I will join her shortly, and it would be very unwise on her part to attempt to bolt the door this time. I bid you goodnight Sarah."

Anne lay motionless on the furthest edge of the great bed, terrified to move a muscle for fear of attracting Henry's attention. The
ache in her throat was becoming intolerable and her eyes smarted
with tears. Vaguely she remembered her mother's useless advice to
her daughters: "Be sensible; if you weep he will be angry. A man
does not care for a sobbing bride." It was not fear of her husband's
anger which made Anne suppress any outward sign of her misery,
only the fear that any sound or movement of hers might awaken
him, and cause him to resume his love-making. He slept? Surely
he slept sound now, his breathing was deep—almost a snore, she
thought with disgust. Cautiously she moved slightly, relaxing her
rigid limbs, hatefully aware of their nakedness beneath the covers.
If only she could find her gown she would feel better. The room
was close and airless. Feeling as though held and bound by soft
invisible cords, she suddenly took a deep breath and half rose from
the pillows.

Henry moved immediately and stifling a sob she sank back as his
hand reached out and touched her. Tense, despairing, she waited
as it slowly moved down her arm to her finger-tips and then gently,
caressingly, began its inevitable journey back again until it came to
rest on her breast.

"You are cold my love, put on your gown," Henry murmured
sleepily, and turned away from her taking most of the covers with
him. He was almost instantly asleep but had time to reflect wryly
that he might have made the same observation an hour earlier,
though the donning of a gown would in no way have improved the
situation then.

As Anne groped for it, and hastily struggled into its comforting
folds, she felt for the first time a small spark of gratitude to her
husband.

THE FIRST weeks of life at Bryanston were very pleasant and even the reluctant bride could find little of which to complain except perhaps of too little to do. Laetitia had handed over the keys and household responsibilities that went with them with immense relief. Here there was none of the domestic jealousies which so often arose when a new bride came to her husband's home where a mother or sister was already installed. In any case they were only a token, for the Manor teemed with servants and the housekeeper and steward managed them all very efficiently. Henry's mother having lived mostly at Pylle, they were accustomed to running the household with little reference to the Mistress. Sarah too found herself with more time on her hands than.ever in her life before. It was very different from High Hall where she had been at the beck and call of the three daughters. For Laetitia she did nothing. Henry's sister had her own maid, an elderly woman, who had been the girl's nurse and was in turn bullied and cajoled by her charge whom she blindly adored and in whom she could see no fault.

At first Sarah enjoyed the novelty of so much leisure but as it was spent doing nothing more exciting than keeping Anne company with a piece of fine sewing or tapestry with no real outlet for her energies, after a while she began to get restless. Sometimes from the garden or her window she watched Laetitia enviously as she rode out on her pretty sprightly mare, always with the same young groom in attendance.

Sarah found she was beginning to wonder a little about Laetitia and this handsome young groom. Not that either Anne or Henry seemed to find it at all remarkable. Sarah chided herself both for speculating on the behaviour of others and dwelling too much on her own emotions, which she did increasingly for Henry was never out of her thoughts, although she saw little of him.

The devil finds work for idle hands she reminded herself, yes, and for idle minds too, no doubt. But what to do about it? Poor Sarah, sometimes her toes tingled with frustration and she had to fight down a desire to shout or scream as she sat hour after hour with her gentle mistress, who after her initial hysterical revolt against her marriage had sunk back into a mood of placid resignation, keeping her thoughts and feelings to herself as she had

done all her life.   When Sarah could escape she went for long walks
in the woods and on the hills, which she came to love, but Anne
disapproved highly of this, being convinced that a robber or a
ravisher lurked behind every tree beyond the confines of the
gardens.

They had come to Bryanston in June and the long lazy summer
days slipped by uneventfully until near the end of a particularly
hot August, when Sarah received an unexpected visitor. On being
told that someone was asking for Sarah Godwyn and awaiting her in
the courtyard, she hurried down wondering who in the world
could be inquiring for her. She found her visitor was a man, a
stout jovial person wearing a good cloth coat and spotless white
linen. He was standing gossiping in a friendly fashion with the
steward as she approached.

"Josiah here claims he be kin to you, Mistress Sarah," the
steward told her as she made her bob to the stranger, and with this
casual introduction left them together. Sarah looked at the man
with renewed interest for she was unaware of the existence of any
living relative.

He was a man of fifty or thereabouts, ruddy-faced, with greying
hair and the brightest blue eyes she had ever seen, which twinkled
down at her in the kindest fashion.

"So you are Sarah," he said, at last, having regarded her as
closely as she had him. "And what a pretty wench you've grown
to be," he went on. "Too comely by far to please your poor father.
Perhaps it is as well he did not live to be plagued by the sight of a
beautiful daughter."

He shook his head in mock sorrow. "He would not have
approved. No, he would not have approved at all, no more than he
did of his brother who stands before you."

Sarah had to laugh at his lugubrious expression which sat so
oddly on his broad, good-humoured face.

"Is that really true sir," she asked a little doubtfully. "Are you
my own uncle? Why, I did not know I had any living kin."

She did not add that she found it almost inconceivable that this
merry gentleman, with his air of enjoying life to the full, could
possibly be own brother to the father she remembered; a gaunt,
soberly clad figure, who seemed to spend every waking hour wres-
tling with his own and his neighbours' sins, real or imagined;
preaching eternal damnation every Sunday in the Meeting House.
As a small child Sarah had sometimes wondered if it was really
worthwhile to try so hard to be good, because sooner or later you

were bound to slip up and the final punishment would be just the same as if you had been naughty all the time and enjoyed it.

Josiah assured her that he was indeed full brother to her late father but his life had taken a very different course. He had discovered very soon that he was temperamentally unsuited to quiet village life in general and in particular with the restrictions of the Society of Friends, of which his family were the leading spirits. So at the age of fifteen he had set off for Poole and the wider horizons offered by a seafaring life which he had found far more to his taste.

Sarah nodded understandingly. She was immediately aware that her Uncle Josiah was the embodiment of what an English Sea Captain should be although she had never to her knowledge met one before.

He went on to tell her that he was now retired, mostly to please his wife, and had bought the lease of an Inn in the neighbouring village of Durweston.

The life suited him tolerably well, the Inn was on the Sherborne road and there were plenty of travellers coming and going to make life interesting still.

"Aye, my dear," he smiled at her, "the roles are just reversed. Now I sit in 'port' and the world comes to me. My customers are like ships, calling in to be rested and refreshed bringing news and tales of other places before they set forth again. Some return again and again, some disappear into the night and are gone forever."

Sarah found that she liked him more and more as he talked in his easy friendly fashion. He was like a great breath of fresh salt air blowing suddenly through her narrow closeted life and the thought that someone so vital, travelled and worldly, claimed her as his own niece gave her a feeling of belonging, which made her feel warm and happy inside. It was as if a place had been filled which had been empty for too long, and the cold fingers of her father's disapproval could not touch it. It was probably the first time that Sarah had consciously rejected the opinion of her pious parent whose teachings had guided almost every facet of her daily life.

She accepted with pleasure Josiah's invitation to visit "The Sign of the Gate" and meet her aunt as soon as she could get leave from Anne to do so, and Josiah told her she must look on it as her home where she would be welcome to come and go as she pleased. Before they parted, Josiah tilted up Sarah's face and asked permission, as her only relative, to give her a kiss.

"I don't mind telling you Sarah," he said, "I have been putting off this visit. I was scared that any daughter of Amos would be a long sour-faced piece who'd quickly send me about me business. But I might have known you'd take after your mother. I was almost sorry I'd gone away to sea when I came home and saw what Amos had got for himself. Aye lovely, she was with her corn-coloured hair and they queer yellow-green eyes like yer own. I'd a known you anywhere by those eyes. But your father, God rest his soul, he couldn't abear beauty, sinful he thought it was. He wouldn't nourish it and tend it, not him. Ignore it, forget it— cover it up, hide it away. He starved it, that's what he did. Beauty must be fed, it thrives on love and admiration—that's the food it needs. The last time I saw your mother you were a wee mite and she was a pale shadow of what she'd been. He'd made her a shroud before her time."

Sarah was thoughtful as she returned to the house. Josiah's words had made her see her mother in a new light. She remembered her as a gentle, timid person, always in the background. She found it difficult even to recall her features, whereas every line of her father's solemn long face and hawklike eyes with their glint of fanaticism was engraved on her memory. He must have been a great deal older than his wife, she realised, and indeed her mother must have been still a young woman when she quietly slipped out of this life within a month of her dominating husband's death. Perhaps he had ordered her to follow and obedient to the end she had done so.

Sarah shuddered. For her faith and loyalty her mother had received few rewards in this life.

In the privacy of her little room, Sarah looked at her own reflection in a small piece of mirror. She saw round smooth cheeks, a full generous mouth, a tip-tilted nose and wide-set eyes which changed colour according to the tricks of light from green to amber. It did not seem possible that the grey shadowy figure she remembered as her mother could ever have looked like this, glowing with youthful vitality.

10 'The Sign of the Gate'

SARAH WASTED no time in telling Anne about her unexpected visitor and new found relative, and her mistress gladly gave her permission to visit Captain Godwyn and his wife the very next day. Durweston village lay less than two miles up the valley from Bryanston and it was a very pleasant walk on a summer afternoon along the tree-shaded road following the course of the river which ran at the foot of a steep bank.

Sarah set off with a light heart, wearing her best dress, cut much lower than she was used to for it was one that Anne had given to her. The addition of a snowy white kerchief round her shoulders and tucked into the neck both improved its appearance and satisfied her own modesty. For once she had discarded the severe puritan cap which usually concealed her bright hair and instead, a dainty confection of lace and ribbon charmingly and inadequately covered her red-gold curls.

She soon reached the village and looked for someone to direct her to the Inn, but there seemed to be nobody about. The cob and thatched cottages with their overhanging eaves almost concealing the upper windows dozed like sleepy brown mice in the sunshine. It seemed a pity to disturb them, Sarah thought, by knocking on doors, so she wandered on through the quiet village street, inhaling the summer smell of new mown grass, the scent of thyme and cottage garden flowers, mixed with pungent whiffs of wood smoke, and the sweet sour smell of horses and cattle as she passed an open byre.

She came at last to the Inn and found it was the last house in the village. The reason for its name was evident for just beyond there was a gate across the road where it started to climb again towards the open down.

Her feeling of sudden shyness as she knocked on the broad oak door was soon banished when it was swiftly opened and she found herself swept into the huge embrace of a rosy-cheeked smiling body who could be none other than Mistress Godwyn.

That first afternoon at "The Sign of the Gate" was a unique experience for Sarah. Never before could she remember an occasion when she was the centre of interest and attention. Her appearance, her dress, her hair, her pretty face, all received their

full share of comment and admiration, and she was plied with
sweetmeats and goodies almost from the moment she stepped into
the cosy panelled parlour, where even on this warm day a few logs
smouldered and flickered on the huge hearth stone.

To Sarah, used as she was to living always in other people's
houses with not one single soul, since her parents' death, to whom
she could feel she belonged, it was overwhelming. Usually independent and self-sufficient, happy enough and not consciously
aware of what was missing in her life, the kindness and warm
welcome of her new found relatives pierced the armour of her
reserve, brought unaccustomed tears to her eyes and a warm glow
of love for everyone about her.

When it was time to leave, Josiah and her Aunt Loveday insisted
that Damon Hardy, the son of a local farmer, should escort her back
to Bryanston. The young man had called to see her uncle on farm
business, and had been pressed to stay and eat with them. Most of
the time he had sat silently gazing at Sarah with obvious admiration, looking hastily away whenever he caught her eye. Sarah's
protests that she was well able to take care of herself on the short
walk home went unheeded. The Godwyn's were determined to
guard and cherish their new found niece and neither Sarah nor
Damon had any say in the matter. As she kissed her aunt and uncle
goodbye she was amused to detect an unmistakeable matchmaking
gleam in their eyes.

Looking up at the young man beside her as they set off and
wondering what they would find to talk about, she was suddenly
reminded of Henry, and realised that for the first time in weeks she
had not given him a thought all day. The excitement of this rare
outing had for once banished him from her mind, but only temporarily. Now she felt she could not wait to get back to the Manor
House where there was always the chance of seeing him. On such
glimpses was her love for him still fed although she conscientiously
tried to avoid him as a rule. Now after her happy day, feeling the
affections of her own family wrapped about her like a cloak, her
secret love for Henry, far from seeming less important, burned more
fiercely within her than ever before.

It was almost dark when Sarah and Damon reached the stable
entrance and here Sarah informed her escort that he could safely
leave her. She would slip through the yard and into the house in a
moment and must hurry for her mistress might need her. She
waited politely whilst the shy young man stumbled through a few
sentences of regret that they must part so soon and of his hopes of

seeing her again. Listening to him Sarah had gathered that he was the only son and would in time take over his father's excellent farm. A better match for herself would be hard to find, but as she listened her only emotion was one of slight gratification, and looking up at him she found herself admiring his youthful good looks with the objectivity of a sister or a much older woman.

As they stood there, Damon reluctant to take his leave and Sarah impatient to get away, Henry rode into the yard. He hailed the boy in a friendly fashion as he dismounted and tossed the reins to a waiting groom. As they stood in conversation for a moment, the talk mostly about the coverts and chances of a good shooting season, Sarah was hesitant whether to stay or go. Finally she murmured her farewells to Damon and set off towards the house. Henry followed and caught her up almost immediately. She felt his arm slip round her waist and heard his lazy drawl in her ear.

"So—what a pretty young man you've found Sarah," he whispered, "he is a fine lad, Damon, you could do worse."

"Your pardon, Sir, he is but an acquaintance. We met for the first time today," Sarah replied crossly.

"What odds does that make, there has to be a first time, and pretty as you are looking I warrant it'll not be the last. He could not take his eyes from you."

Gently Sarah disengaged herself. "Forgive me Sir, I must go. I have been absent since noon, visiting my uncle and aunt in Durweston." In these last words there was a new note of childish self-importance.

Henry grinned and made her a formal bow.

"So Sarah Godwyn has found more than one protector today. I must be warned. But do not worry, I'll not plague you, I like you too well little Godwyn."

He gave her curls a playful tug and admonished her to run and find her mistress. "I know well she is loathe to have you out of her sight," he added, "and who can blame her?"

The house struck chill after the warmth of the summer evening out of doors, and it seemed as if all the happiness of her lovely day drained away as she entered, leaving her empty and cold inside. For a moment she felt physically sick.

He did not care one tiny bit for her; gladly he would see her married to Damon Hardy, leave his house, go away down the valley and perhaps never set eyes on her again. He would scarcely notice her absence. There would always be a pretty wench amongst the minions at Bryanston, who he could tease, whose curls he could pull, and who would amuse him for a moment and some no doubt who would willingly give him additional pleasures which Amos Godwyn's daughter could never contemplate.

Then, what was she thinking of, she asked herself. It was no matter for regret that Henry did not return her love. If it were so even in the smallest degree, what then? How much more difficult to avoid temptation, if Henry realled wanted her. Could she then trust herself not to commit what she knew to be a deadly sin?

She could hear her father's voice after all these years. Words, horrible words, which were always on his tongue. They echoed hollowly inside her head, just as they had echoed round the white-washed walls of the little Meeting House at Wimborne. "A woman taken in adultery!" Sarah hurried through the dark passages, and tried to put these thoughts from her. What had she to fear, she had learnt her lesson well, her father's teachings had been drilled into her and just as his voice was still in her head she was sure that his eyes were still upon her. But some prop, some stay, had collapsed under her today. She was no longer so sure, so strong in her beliefs. In imagination she was back again in the cosy parlour of the Inn at Durweston, where she could smell the mingled scent of wood smoke and baking bread, and see again the laden table, the hams and cheeses and the overflowing tankards of home-brewed beer. Her Uncle Josiah's hearty laugh drove out her father's voice. She could see his great stomach shaking, hear again his merry tales, punctuated with winks and nods, and often left unfinished when he was shushed by Aunt Loveday, who sat smiling indulgent-ly, her broad plain face beautiful in its kindly contentment. "He is a bad man," she had told Sarah severely, "No woman was safe with him, but I have him tied here now." How happy they were, and indeed, they must always have been. Whatever Josiah had done, Sarah was sure he had never hurt Aunt Loveday. Now, to her they had given the most truly happy day she ever remembered. And of that her father would have disapproved.

It was all very puzzling. The trouble is, thought Sarah seriously, it is going to be difficult to spend the rest of my life knowing that I am not only my father's daughter but also Josiah's niece.

Sarah was jerked out of her reverie when she entered her mis-tress's boudoir. She found Anne reclining on a couch, looking very white and ill with two of the young chambermaids fussing around her pressing cold rags to her head and waving burnt feathers under her nose in such incompetent fashion that they were soon likely to singe her hair. It was stiflingly hot in the room, which facing south had had the full benefit of the sun all day. The window was tight shut now against the night air and all the candles were alight. The heat and the disgusting smell of the burnt feathers caught at Sarah's throat. Without asking any questions she sent one maid to open the window and told the other to remove herself and her dangerous remedies immediately from the room. Then she knelt down beside her mistress.

Anne looked at her with relief.

"Thank God, you are returned Sarah. I could not have tolerated their clumsy ministrations a moment longer."

"Tell me ma'am, what happened, are you sick? Did you fall in a faint?"

Anne nodded. "I had been in the still-room, they were boiling the jam and somehow the smell made me feel sick. I could not stay. I left and walked a little by the river. I felt quite well again, and then . . ."

Sarah had stopped listening, she did not need to hear any more. The candle flames flickered into strange shapes moved by the gentle breeze from the open window, they grew tall and thin as if trying to reach the ceiling, then darted sidways to twist and turn like dancers. Sarah's eyes were on them but she did not see them. Anne's voice murmured on softly, hesitant and worried.

She does not know, thought Sarah, does not even guess. How strange it all was. Were she in Anne's place, how happy she would be, how hopeful, how lightly to the servants would she dismiss a little swoon. The heat, of course. Hoping no one would guess before she herself was sure. Hugging her glorious secret, longing for and yet delaying the moment when she would tell Henry.

She sighed and looked down at Anne. The colour was coming back into her cheeks. Her clear blue eyes, a little anxious, looked into Sarah's, the smooth pale gold hair loose on the pillow made a perfect frame against the milk white skin. Anne looked a little fragile, but very beautiful and no longer ill.

Sarah supposed that in all kindness she should reassure her, but she could find no words. No, let someone else tell Henry's wife that she was probably already carrying the son he desired so much.

Sarah rose to her feet.

"Come, let me help you to undress ma'am, you must go to your bed. Tomorrow we will call in the doctor from Blandford, if you wish, but I feel sure 'tis nothing. It was just the heat."

11 Sarah's excuses and Henry's heir

DURING ANNE'S pregnancy Sarah had no time to be bored. The elaborate preparations instigated by Henry for this long awaited heir kept the entire household busy. Improvements which Henry had itched to make from the moment he came into his inheritance were set in train immediately causing a great deal of inconvenience and upset to everyone with very little result. The big rambling house seemed to absorb and swallow up all modern renovations like a hungry old wolf whose appetite was never appeased, but whose condition was but little improved by its new diet. It was only the near approach of winter with its inevitable floods that prevented Henry from immediately starting on his pet project of diverting the river into the side stream furthest from the house, always having been convinced that its proximity was unhealthy.

Whenever she had the opportunity Sarah would slip down to Durweston to see the Godwyns, where a warm welcome always awaited her. Whether by chance or design Damon Hardy was often there and usually took her home riding pillion on his horse. On one or two occasions he produced a mount for Sarah to ride which she enjoyed enormously. Sometimes she felt very guilty in the face of the knowing looks and smiles of her uncle and aunt and Damon's shy attentions. She knew full well what the outcome would be, but by sustaining a manner of cool reserve towards the boy, managed to delay it as long as possible. Fortunately, Damon's courtship was not precipitous. He was a true countryman, content to prepare the ground and bide his time patiently. It was spring again before he asked Sarah to marry him and he had already consulted and won the approval of both Josiah and his own parents.

She had long expected his declaration but when it came it threw Sarah into a panic. Although she knew she should say yes, and would probably regret it for evermore if she did not, she nevertheless found it impossible to do so. The imminent arrival of Anne's child gave her an excuse to stall. He must ask her again when the baby had safely arrived; she could think of nothing till then; her first duty was to her Mistress. Damon was hurt and puzzled. He could not understand any of her reasons. What was to stop her saying yes? He wasn't asking her to marry him immediately. Unlike some they had no cause to wed in haste. She need not yet tell her Mistress if the idea of losing Sarah would upset her Ladyship at this time. In fact so far as nice plodding Damon was concerned the cycle was complete, his courtship had been conducted rightly and properly, and he was disconcerted to find that Sarah was not playing her part. Sarah was sorry but adamant in refusing to give him a definite answer. On the other hand she allowed him the kiss he demanded and had obviously looked forward to, expecting that it would seal their pledge, and she was surprised to find the experience not unpleasant. Nor was this lost on Damon who went away feeling more hopeful and convinced that Sarah's reluctance was mere feminine coquetry.

Later Damon confided in Josiah, who made light of his fears and encouraged him in his hopes.

"She'll come around Damon lad, never fear," Josiah told him. "There's a lass that should be married and soon. A good wife and a warm bedfellow she'll make ye too," he went on, "or I'm no judge of women. Even brother Amos could not have suppressed the spirit in young Sarah. 'Tis all a part of it, she wants to keep you dangling." These last words, sent Damon away with much to think about. "Don't let her play with you too long lad; there'll be others soon enough as eager for her as yourself. Don't waste your time. 'Tis spring, the woods be dry and warm and a mossy bank makes a fine couch, so I'm told," he said with a broad wink. "Get her in the family way lad; she'll marry you soon enough then. What's the harm in it, you mean to do the right thing. If she cannot make up her own mind, make it up for her and that's the best way to do it."

Any intentions Damon may have had of acting immediately on this advice however, were defeated by Sarah who carefully avoided being alone with him and whose visits to "The Sign of the Gate' became less frequent as the time for her Mistress's confinement drew near.

Anne's child was born in May just one year after her marriage to Henry. The baby was a boy. A son and an heir in the direct line; the first for nearly a hundred years.

Anne, happier than she had ever been since she came to Bryanston was pampered and spoilt by everyone, and Henry could not do enough to please her. Proud and delighted with her son as any mother who had conceived and carried her child with love and longing for his arrival, she had in fact, loathed every day of her pregnancy and had looked forward to her confinement with dread and fear. Sarah, who had been by her side constantly throughout the long months of waiting, never ceased to be surprised that her gentle kindly mistress had not only remained cool and indifferent to her husband but seemed to take the same attitude towards his child as it grew within her. Her one consolation apparently lay in the fact that it enabled her to use it as an excuse to bar Henry from her bed from the earliest possible moment.

The baby's arrival however wrought an enormous change. From the first moment he was put into her arms, Anne doted on the boy and seemed to look upon him as a miraculous gift from heaven in which she herself had had no part. Henry's patience and good humour with his wife had never faltered and in the son and heir he had so much wanted they at last found a mutual interest which created a more relaxed and affectionate ambience between them. Henry, however, soon discovered that it would never be more than that on Anne's side. All the love she had to give would be lavished on this scrap of humanity which passively and unwillingly she had helped to create. Her natural woman's instincts towards the opposite sex—withheld, warped and misunderstood for too long—now at last found an outlet. As she had loved her father, now she loved her son, but the barrier between herself and her husband remained impenetrable.

After the baby's birth Sarah was busier than ever, for not only was Anne in a very delicate state of health but also she would entrust the supervision of her child to nobody but Sarah.

The doctors had shaken their heads solemnly over Anne's condition and had advised against her having another child for some years. Disappointed as Henry undoubtedly was he accepted this disagreeable knowledge philosophically. At least he had his heir and fortunately young Henry William was a fine healthy baby. Assured of this, and that his wife and child were in good hands, Henry decided that it was time he rode down to Somerset to inspect his estates there. In his absence Anne gradually regained her health and in her motherhood gained a new confidence and importance which had been lacking in her previously. The news that it was advisable that she should have no more children had been broken gently to her and probably nobody but Sarah knew or guessed how much she secretly rejoiced in the knowledge.

Henry had been away some weeks. Anne was happy and much occupied with her son when Sarah began to think seriously about Damon's proposal. It was the obvious and sensible course for her to accept it, and she felt she had better give him an opportunity as soon as possible to ask her again. With Henry away the days were endless and there seemed to be nothing to look forward to, denied as she was, even the pleasurable misery of the few glimpses she had of him when he was at Bryanston. Sarah did not analyse her feelings but if she had she would have realised that, like other victims of a hopeless love, the misery caused by the loved one's presence was infinitely preferable to the dull emptiness of his absence. An emptiness somehow had to be filled. Now with Anne well again Sarah found herself once more with time on her hands, and she decided to visit Josiah and Loveday at the Inn and if Damon were there, she would let events take their course.

Her uncle and aunt were delighted to see her and especially pleased to hear that for once this was not to be a brief visit. Melody, who had been sent for from High Hall and proved to be an efficient nurse, was in charge of the baby and there was no need for Sarah to hurry back. Her aunt plied her with good food and her uncle with all the titbits of local gossip about which some of his comments were so outrageous that Sarah found herself choking with laughter and more relaxed and happy than she had felt for weeks. When Damon called in as if by accident just before she was due to take her leave, Sarah, with that warm glow inside her induced not only by the kindness and affection of her relatives but also by the new home brew which Josiah had insisted upon her sampling, greeted him with more pleasure than was her habit, and accepted without demur his offer to walk back to Bryanston with her.

They were both in high spirits when they eventually set off. Possibly Josiah's latest brew was more potent than usual, and Damon's tankard had been filled more than once by his generous host before he was allowed to leave.

Sarah was not surprised when Damon suggested leaving the dusty road and taking what he called a short cut through the woods. If no shorter it was certainly more pleasant than the road which was busy tonight with the waggons and horses of farmers and cottagers returning from the market. They climbed a steep narrow ride which brought them to the top of the hanging woods where Sarah collapsed exhausted, saying she could not walk a step further for the moment. As Damon sank down beside her she took one look at his serious young face, then hastily looked away and prattled quickly on about the magnificence of the view down through the trees to the valley.

Well, she thought, she had deliberately allowed him his opportunity, and it was too late to retreat now. If he still wanted her, her answer this time would have to be a definite yes or no. For a while Damon sat silently beside her not quite knowing what to do, terrified of making a false move and losing her forever. His first proposal had been carefully rehearsed, if clumsily delivered. Now he was at a loss as to how to proceed and far less sure of himself than he had been on that occasion. Finally he slipped an arm tentatively around her waist and when she did not immediately repulse him, grew bolder and pulled her towards him. Words, suddenly, did not seem necessary. She was in his arms, yielding and unresistant, and with a flood of relief Damon was convinced that Josiah was right, speech was unnecessary and useless for such as he, and action was undoubtedly to be preferred. Sarah, in a mood of resignation, allowed him to kiss her; expecting that he would soon release her and once more beg her to marry him. She was very much surprised when instead of doing so his advances became more and more passionate until she found herself pushed down full length on the soft leafy carpet and almost helpless in his embrace. She struggled to extricate herself, just a little alarmed at the young man's unexpected passion, but confident that she could quell his ardour with a look or a word, even if her futile struggles were no match for his superior strength. For the moment his mouth was hard on hers and she could not speak, then suddenly she no longer wanted to. With the whole length of Damon's ardent young body against her own, the will to resist deserted her. There was a weakness, a strange melting in her limbs and a terrifying reluctance to do anything other than respond to his desire. When minutes later she murmured his name it was in a tone of surprise.

"'Tis all right Sarah love, there'll be no harm done, we'll be wed soon as you like, but I'll wait no longer." If Damon had kept quiet at that moment the whole course of Sarah's life might have been different. They would have made love as naturally as the wild creatures of the woods in whose territory they lay and later back in their own world of man-made houses, laws and conventions, would have had their union blessed and acknowledged in the sight of the people amongst whom they must live out their lives. Instead, his soft country voice muffled in her hair, shocked Sarah into a realisation of what she was about to do. Her senses had taken over for a wild moment, but she was not going to let them betray her mindlessly into an action which would have such long reaching results. Confused and bewildered, horrified at her physical response to

Damon when it was Henry whom she loved, she pushed the boy away from her and sat up.

To Sarah's relief, Damon was surprised at this sudden reversal and made no attempt to restrain her. She was not in the mood for an undignified scuffle and felt that if he so much as touched her again at this moment she would sink her teeth into his hand.

She was right in thinking that she was capable of controlling her erstwhile shy young lover. The real danger had lain hidden and unsuspected in herself.

Damon got up and strolled away for a moment. When he came back and sat down some little distance from her he looked sulky and slightly ashamed. Inexperienced as she was, Sarah was sensitive and honest enough too, to realise that he had a right to be vexed with her and that she was the one who should be ashamed of her conduct.

They sat wordlessly for a while, carefully avoiding each other's eyes. Damon got out his knife and whittled away at a stick as intently as if he were fashioning something of immense importance. The sun had disappeared behind the western hills and the bright daytime colours of the valley were merged into an uniform greyness. The silence was broken by the sharp crackle of a cock pheasant going to roost almost over their heads, followed by the slow clop, clop of a horse's hooves on the road below them.

"He's late abed," Damon said, throwing away his handiwork and peering up into the trees, "and we better get on Sarah or they'll be wondering where you be to."

Sarah's heart was heavy as they walked on. He was so nice, kind and good. He would love and cherish her, what more could she ask or expect. They parted as usual at the stable gates, and there at last Damon found courage to demand an answer to the question which had lain unspoken between them all day.

Sarah, reminding herself that she had set out with the intention of accepting his proposal, knew that nothing was changed except perhaps that the new knowledge of herself, which she had acquired that evening, made it all the more certain that it was the sensible thing to do.

"When shall it be lass?" Damon asked simply. Not without reason, it was for the inarticulate Damon now just a question of naming the day. To Sarah, the question put in this way seemed like a reprieve.

"I will talk to my Lady tomorrow. I must hasten now but will send you word soon."

She was gone and Damon set off back to Durweston, happily convinced that everything was all but settled between them.

For Sarah, however, it was not so simple. She had still not actually said that she would marry him; she had given no promise. With true feminine contrariness, she felt irritated now that Damon had not extracted one from her. She retired as early as possible, anxious to be alone with her thoughts, which, incomfortable as they were, had to be faced. She realised that in some strange way it was her frustrated desire for Henry which had made her so responsive to Damon's lovemaking, just as it was, paradoxically, the thought of Henry going out of her life forever that had made her repulse him before it was too late.

Not for one moment had she given a thought to the sin she was about to commit—the sin with the long ugly name which she had been brought up to regard as standing higher on a lengthy list than most of the others. It was this that she found so alarming. It was as if the person she thought she knew herself to be had suddenly abandoned her body and left it defenceless. Restless, unable to sleep Sarah finally decided to tell Anne tomorrow that she and Damon wanted to marry as soon as possible. She would also suggest that she stayed with the Godwyns until the arrangements could be made. In that way she was unlikely to see Henry, who was not expected to return for some weeks, and could put him out of her mind forever. She slept at last, glad that she had finally made her decision, sadly convinced that though she had in her the makings of a wanton, Damon could yet save her and the sooner she married him the better it would be for her immortal soul.

12   Sarah and Henry

THE NEXT morning Sarah took the first opportunity of telling her Mistress that she wished to marry Damon Hardy, sure that by doing so the whole matter would be shared by others, out of her hands, and settled forever.

What she had not reckoned with was Anne's reaction to her news. She was plainly aghast at the thought of losing her young companion and determined to dissuade her.

"But Sarah, I thought you loved Bryanston, more indeed than I myself. You have a pleasant life. Why should you wish to change it? What can this farmer boy give you that you do not have here with us?"

Sarah regarded Anne helplessly. In what language that Anne would understand could she explain. It seemed that all the natural desires and emotions of a young woman had never troubled her Mistress for a moment and she was apparently incapable of imagining them in someone else.

Tentatively Sarah pointed out that it was not unusual, quite the contrary in fact, for a young woman to wish to marry and have a home and children of her own.

"You mean it is usually necessary for her to do so. In your case that does not apply. You are comfortable here and welcome to stay with me as long as you wish, and you are fortunate in that you have no Mama to force you into marriage."

"But Ma'am, surely you do not think that every girl has to be forced, just because that was your own unhappy experience," Sarah replied with some exasperation.

"No indeed, I am not so stupid, but there can be but one other reason. That you love this . . . this bumpkin and that I refuse to believe. Why you have scarcely mentioned his name or troubled to see him of late and you certainly have not the air of a lovesick maid, my dear Sarah, so why, why should you wish to leave me? It is evident that you do not at all concern yourself with my feelings."

Sarah was silent. She could think of no answer. Everything Anne had said was irrefutable, her mistress could have no inkling of her true reason, nor quite obviously could Sarah disclose or even give a hint of it to Anne of all people.

Pleased to think she had made her point and recovered from her first alarm Anne was now prepared to dismiss the whole matter.

"Now put this silly idea out of your mind and send Master Damon about his business. I need you Sarah, I have no friend in this house but you,. I give you my word that if you wish to marry later you shall have my help to make a far better match. I do not doubt but that I could persuade Mr. Portman to give you a substantial dowry." She sighed: "Whatever else, he is entirely generous."

Sarah was about to speak, firmly determined not to have her own decision, over which she had battled so painfully, lightly swept aside. "Ma'am I assure you . . ." she started, but Anne interrupted her.

"Enough now, there is much to do. I received a message but an hour ago, Mr. Portman is returning sooner than expected and will be here by dinner time today. I was about to tell you but your news put it quite out of my mind."

Sarah listened quietly while Anne gave her various orders. This intelligence set her heart racing. Even if Anne had permitted it, she was no longer anxious to continue the conversation. Everything seemed to conspire against her good intentions and to shake her resolve. With Anne set against her marriage, and Henry home again before she could absent herself, would she be able to keep to her decision, she wondered.

During the next few days Sarah both carefully avoided Henry and tried hard to reopen the subject of her marriage with Anne but with no success. Every day that passed made the whole situation worse and Sarah had never been more unhappy in her life. Wracked with indecision, her resentment against Anne grew. If only she had had her Mistress's blessing she would have given Damon the answer he wanted immediately. The Godwyn's would have been delighted to make all arrangements and there would have been no going back. It was in this mood of despair and frustration that Sarah escaped from the house one evening and walked miserably along the lonely river path towards Blandford. The weather was oppressive and there was thunder in the air. Sarah's nerves were taut and almost at breaking point. If only there were someone in whom she could confide, someone who would sympathise and understand, advise and direct her. It was as she retraced her steps back towards the house that she saw Henry coming towards her. There was no escape, the wooded cliff rose steeply on one side and on her right was the river. Inevitably they met face to face on the narrow path. With a brief curtsey and a murmured "Good evening

Sir," Sarah made an attempt to pass him but Henry obviously had
no intention of allowing her to do so, and firmly blocked the way.
To make things worse his companion, a spaniel puppy whom
Sarah had played with in his absence, leapt upon her with yelps of
delight.

"My dog has excellent taste I see and a most delightful and
uninhibited manner of showing his affection," Henry remarked.
At that moment there was a distant roll of thunder. The little dog
stood still for a moment, then with his short tail tucked firmly
between his legs and long ears flying he turned and bolted for
home. The fast disappearing figure looked so comical that Sarah
found herself laughing helplessly whilst Henry watched him go in
open-mouthed dismay.

"Damn, and I had hoped to train him to the gun," he said at last.
Then looking up at the darkening sky, he took Sarah's arm.
"Come, perhaps he has reason and we should follow. You are
thinly clad child and the storm is about to break."

"Now tell me all the news," he went on as they walked, "are you
betrothed to young Hardy yet? I have been absent these two
months, surely even Damon has come to the point by now?"

"He has indeed Sir," Sarah replied in the cool small voice she had
learnt to reserve for her master, "and I had thought to marry him
but my Mistress is reluctant to release me. I owe her a great deal
and do not wish to displease her."

"Lud, Sarah, would she have you remain a maid all your life?"

"Why not? 'Tis what she would have wished for herself."
Sarah spoke quickly, with some bitterness, before she realised to
whom she was speaking, and then glanced a little nervously at her
companion.

Henry smiled down at her quite unmoved.

"Do not worry little Godwyn, that has been evident to me for
some time. You have disclosed nothing that I do not already know.
Your Mistress is amiable and I have a fondness for her but she has
some odd notions on certain subjects, which I feel sure you do not
share any more than I do myself. I think you should marry Damon,
and soon. At least you will not then be here to plague me."

Sarah looked at him in surprise.

"Do I plague you Sir, I was not aware of it."

"A little, yes, I admit you do a little, but I assure you it is in the
nicest possible way."

Sarah looked away in some confusion. She was saved from any
further conversation however by the rain which after a few

warning spots which they had hardly noticed suddenly descended on them in full force.

"Come, we must run, you will be soaked."

Sarah picked up her skirts and followed this excellent advice. The rain was blinding and they had gone no more than a few yards when she stumbled and would have fallen if Henry had not quickly caught hold of her.

It was immediately evident that she was in some pain.

"I fear I have turned my ankle, pray continue Sir," Sarah said, "it is of no use for us both to get drenched."

"Indeed I shall do nothing of the sort. Do you think I should be so ungallant as to leave you." Henry looked about him seeking a shelter. They were still some distance from the house, separated from it by the gardens which on this south side were extensive.

"'Tis of no consequence, I assure you," Sarah protested, "I will follow slowly in a moment or shelter beneath the trees."

"That would be highly dangerous and very foolish with a thunderstorm approaching. No, I have a better idea. The Folly of course, 'tis close by." Without further ado Henry picked her up in his arms and carried her towards the little pavilion, which was just inside the wall enclosing the formal gardens. It was a charming little building, brick built, dry and sunny, reached by a short flight of steps. The windows were above the level of the wall and commanded a view both up and down the valley.

Henry negotiated the short distance swiftly in spite of his burden and ignored Sarah's contention that she was quite capable of hobbling with a little help from him.

"This way is quicker and for my part more enjoyable," he assured her seriously, "and as for yours," he added, "I trust that the pain of being in my arms at least does not exceed the agony of putting even your light weight onto a sprained foot."

With lowered lids and her faced screwed up against the rain, Sarah successfully hid the happiness in her eyes and as Henry mounted the steps her arms went round his neck as if she feared to fall.

Carefully Henry set her down inside, keeping one arm about her, and at that moment a vivid flash of lightning split the gloom of the evening and for a fraction of a second bathed them both and every corner of their sanctuary in an unearthly white light. It was almost immediately followed by a terrific crash of thunder directly overhead. Instinctively Sarah stepped nearer to her companion. When the next flash came she buried her head in Henry's shoulder and he held her close as the thunder cracked again louder than ever, then echoed and rumbled round the neighbouring hills, sounding in Sarah's ears like the familiar voice of an angry old man whose roar of rage silenced all save his own incessant mumbled grumbling, to which she had no wish to listen. As the thunder died away, Henry was agreeably surprised to find that Sarah did not immediately withdraw from his protecting arms. It was no hardship to continue to hold the small damp figure close to him and he had no intention of making the first move toward their parting. When finally she raised her head from his shoulder Henry held her a little closer.

"You are trembling. Are you frightened Sarah?" he asked.

"What should I fear Sir?" she replied softly.

"Why, the thunder of course—what else?"

"No, I do not fear the storm, surely we are safe enough here. I do not think I am frightened now." She smiled up at him and Henry had never seen her look so enchanting. He pushed back a wet strand of her hair which clung to her forehead and removed her usually neat starched cap, now a useless limp rag. Gently, his fingers in her hair, he pulled back her head until she was forced to look up into his eyes.

"You are beautiful Sarah," he said after a moment. "Does Master Hardy tell you so? What a fortunate lad he is to have such a prize within his reach. I protest my dear, t'would be a devilish wicked waste if he did not fully appreciate his good fortune."

"Please, I beg you Sir, let us not speak of Damon. I have told you I shall abide by my Lady's wishes. I do not intend to marry."

"Then you do not love him, or you would not be so easily persuaded," Henry replied with conviction.

Sarah shook her head and made a half-hearted attempt to move away, but Henry's arms tightened around her.

"My sympathies therefore must be with poor Damon," he went on, "but I own that that will not prevent me attempting to console you. With a little encouragement I would dare to kiss you." Without waiting for any, he bent his head and lightly touched her lips with his. He could read no discouragement in her eyes. Her mouth was as soft as a rose, rain wet and far too sweet to abandon after so brief a salute. Henry found it impossible, and kissed her again, this time with more purpose. Her unexpected response was intoxicating. All the good intentions he had had of stealing no more than one innocent kiss fled and were forgotten, together with his previous belief in Sarah's iron-bound puritan virtue and inaccessibility, for if the gentle kisses she returned were inexperienced there was no doubt of her willingness to learn.

It was a long time before they realised that the storm was over. Oblivious of everything but each other, the 'old man' had continued to grumble round the hills with unabated fury, unheeded by the willing prisoners in the pavilion.   Now at last they were aroused by the silence.

A weak shaft of sunlight, slanting through the window, was a harmless intruder for but a moment.   The open doorway was still barred by silver rods of rain which showed no signs of abating.

Sarah wished it would go on for ever.   She did not dare to think, nor remember, any existence outside this small world where she lay in Henry's arms.   Like a child anxious to sleep again and recapture a dream, she closed her eyes tight and gently rubbed her cheek against his.

"Sarah," Henry's voice was soft, his lips brushing her face as he spoke.   "I suppose I should ask your forgiveness.   I do assure you it is not my practice to seduce virgins who live under my protection."

Sarah murmured inaudibly.

"Will you believe me," he went on, "I have truly sought to avoid you for I must own I am a man easily tempted."   Sarah put her hand gently over his mouth.   He kissed it and immediately removed it.

"No, let me plead my case," he said.   "It was the storm which drove you into my arms, but I swear t'was not my intention to so grossly take advantage of it.   Forgive me Sarah, I fear that I allowed myself to doubt your virtue which previously I had not thought to question.   From that moment I was lost, and what is worse I am unrepentant.   Are you angry with me?"

Taking her by the shoulders he held her away from him so that he could see her face.   Sarah smiled at him.   He certainly did not look repentant nor did she wish that he should be.

"You have no need to ask my forgiveness, for you had every reason to doubt my virtue," she replied calmly, "for virtue surely fled from the moment I desired you to make love to me, as indeed I did, and knew full well what I was about."   She sighed and added with a resigned shrug: "No doubt I shall burn in Hell for it but I do not intend to think of that now."

"Lud Sarah, please do not," Henry exclaimed, "it sounds devilish uncomfortable."

He pulled her to him again and tilted up her face to his.

"What a strange little puritan you are!   Seriously, my love, you puzzle me. I never thought to win you so easily."

"Are you reproaching me Sir?"

"No, that would be intolerable, I am merely curious. Forgive me, I should not question the reasons for so desirable a gift. I will not persist, I have ever understood that it is almost impossible for a woman to be both beautiful and good. I should be the last person to reproach you for relinquishing your claims to the latter."

Sarah lowered her eyes so that he should not see the sudden tears that welled up in them, nor the love that she was determined to hide. In the face of his light-hearted acceptance of her, the one thing she dreaded was that he should guess how deeply she felt about him. Let him believe, if he wished, that she was wanton and 'easy'; that if he was her first lover he would certainly not be her last. The truth would make him uncomfortable.

She realised, only too well, that in Henry's life this was no more than an incident. She, however, had not risked her immortal soul for so little. Inexperienced and innocent as Sarah was, her intuition told her that if Henry knew the intensity of her feelings for him he might think it best to avoid her in the future as he had done in the past. She was determined this should not happen. Both her rigid upbringing and her life as a dependent had taught her the art of concealing her innermost feelings. It did not desert her now. When at last she met his eyes, her own were laughing and provocative.

"So you must conclude that I am no better than I should be after all."

"Better? Worse? Who am I to judge?" Henry kissed the tip of her nose.

"I know only that you have the most ridiculous and delicious little nose, the wonder is that you have remainded virtuous so long with such a sad disadvantage, though 'tis by no means the only one you have to contend with."

Softly he kissed her eyes, her cheeks and her mouth, in turn.

"But how is your poor foot?" he said suddenly.

Sarah looked surprised. They had both forgotten the accident which had brought them here.

Cautiously she stretched out her legs and wriggled her ankles.

"It is still a little painful," she said at last. "Do you think I should try to stand on it?"

"No, that would be most unwise." He took one small foot in both his hands and gently massaged the ankle. She let him continue for a while until looking up he caught an amused gleam in her eyes.

"Does that help at all?" he asked.

"Yes indeed, it is very pleasant, but I fear you have the wrong foot."

Henry dropped it without ceremony and they fell laughing into each others arms.   Outside the rain still teemed down, a friendly ally to their imprisonment.

"If this continues," Henry murmured, "the floods will be up and trap us for the night.   Shall you mind?"

Sarah did not reply.   His arms were warm and safe around her. For her part it could rain green devils for a week.

13   Lovers

ON HIS return from Somerset, Henry had informed his lady with goodnatured sarcasm, that she would not long be troubled with his presence.

"As it appears to be the case that we are to be man and wife in nought but name," he told her, "perhaps 'tis as well that there are urgent affairs awaiting my attention in London. I shall remain here no more than the sennight and you may rest assured I shall not trouble you." With elaborate concern he continued to ask after her health and remarked on her good fortune in retaining her good looks in spite of her delicate condition.

Anne received these assurances with ill-concealed relief. She had scarcely dared to hope or expect that her husband would so easily abide by the doctors' advice. Not for the first time Henry had surprised her by behaving contrary to her preconceived notions.

"No doubt he has a woman in town to whom he longs to return," she mused after this interview. "Now that he has got himself a son he fortunately no longer desires me." Disgust, she was sure, was the slight emotion stirred in her by these thoughts. She could not recognise a faint flicker of jealousy.

The weeks passed by however, and Henry, surprisingly, made no further reference to his departure for London. His manner to Anne remained kind and solicitous but increasingly formal. He saw to it that they were rarely alone and her own apartments at Bryanston became as inviolate and private as her bedchamber had been at High Hall. If Anne was puzzled by her husband's change of plan, she did not speak of it to him though Laetitia, who hoped to accompany him, teased him constantly about it. Only on one occasion did Anne remark to Sarah on Henry's continued presence at Bryanston. They were sitting together in Anne's boudoir, busy with the fine needlework which occupied so much of their day. Through the open window the clatter of horses hooves broke the quiet of the summer morning. Anne glanced up and thoughtfully watched her husband riding out of the forecourt.

"I wonder what keeps him here," she said idly. "I am surprised he delays so long."

Sarah, feeling the blood mounting to her face, bent more closely over her work, she could not speak, though indeed no reply was expected of her to this observation. The silence, lasting no more than seconds, seemed endless when to Sarah's intense relief, the door was flung open and Laetitia stormed into the room.

"He is a monster, he will not say when we shall go to Town and he promised me that I might go with him. Soon the Season will be over," she wailed, "and it will be too late." Receiving no response from the two women apparently placidly continuing with their work, Laetitia crossed to the window and angrily watched horse and rider disappearing over the bridge. Turning back she glared at her sister-in-law, determined to hurt someone to relieve her own feelings.

"'Tis my belief he has a mistress, what else should keep him here," she said scornfully.

Sarah white faced now and tense watched for Anne's reaction. Henry's wife raised her head from her tapestry and looked calmly into the angry eyes staring down at her.

"It is possible," she replied without emotion. With a slight shrug, her head bent once more over her work she added, "Sarah did I not hear the baby?"

Outwardly calm but with fast beating heart, Sarah rose and thankfully escaped into the adjoining room. There she paused for a moment listening to the voices of the two ladies next door fearing that further remarks from Laetitia might point a finger at herself. Little more was said, however, before the slam of a door that undoubtedly signalled the volatile Laetitia's departure. Going to the crib, she gently picked up the child. His whimpering stopped immediately and from the tiny face, Henry's eyes—softly brown, warm and content—stared up at her. She cuddled him close, her cheek against his. "I love you," she whispered. "I wish, I wish that you were mine." With the baby in her arms she returned to her mistress outwardly completely composed. Inwardly she was shaking. For the first time the reality of her situation had been shown clearly to her. She was Henry's mistress. For weeks now they had been lovers.

Henry had not allowed their first impulsive love-making, born of a summer storm, to end with its passing. Before they left the Folly he had made Sarah promise to meet him there the following night and thereafter it had become a regular meeting place. In Sarah he had found a delightful and desirable mistress and he now had no intention of taking the risk of losing her to Damon Hardy or anyone else by going away too soon. Sarah was in love with Henry and once she had given herself to him there was no going back. Nor

did she wish to.   Once defied, all the moral precepts of her puritanical upbringing had to be suppressed, impossible though they were
to sweep out of her mind completely.   In defence she had been
living in a fantasy world where her happiness with Henry had a
dreamlike quality having nothing to do with her own or anyone
else's everyday life.

Laetitia's remarks had shocked and frightened her; yet her one
thought as she busied herself for the rest of the day was of meeting
Henry later in the Folly.

He was there when she arrived and relief flood through her as she
paused on the threshold regarding him.   As he stepped towards her
she reach out to him.

"Please, hold my hand," she whispered.   Henry, who had been
about to take her in his arms, hesitated, then took both her hands
and held them closely against his breast gently pulling her to him.
For a moment she stood with lowered head holding tightly to him
then turned to gaze out into the starlit night. "It is so beautiful,"
she murmured.

"And so I recollect are you", Henry replied, "but am I not
allowed to see your face?   What's wrong?" he added softly.

"Nothing, nothing at all," smiling now, she reached up and
kissed him.   "Come out and look at the stars, the air is so fresh and
I have been closed in the house all day."

Later that night, not for the first time, Henry tried to persuade
her to come to his own apartments in the house but Sarah remained
adamant.

"Laetitia already suspects that you have a mistress here," she
told him.   "In the house there may be prying eyes and gossiping
tongues to spoil everything."   She paused and was thoughtful for a
moment.   "It must not be spoilt," she went on defiantly, "what I
am doing is wrong, I know that well, but to betray your wife under
her own roof, risking that she might come to know of it, that would
seem to me an unforgivable sin."

Henry, who regarded the situation more practically, looked at
her quizzically as he replied. "My wife, dear Sarah, has never set
foot in my bed chamber and would be only too happy if I never
again entered her own.   So damn, what's the odds?   Furthermore,
what will happen when the nights grow cold?   Forgive me, love,
but would you have me freeze to death so that you may preserve a
few remaining puritian prejudices?"

Sarah refused to discuss this point.   The winter was still a long
way off and she had no wish to think so far ahead.   Convinced that

his love for her could only be shortlived, when winter came would he still want her? Anne's coldness and preoccupation with her child may have helped to stifle her own conscience but Henry needed no such excuse. It was obvious that he had ever taken his pleasures lightly and would continue to do so.

In the meanwhile their meetings in the Folly had a magic quality, there they had a small world of their own where all else could be forgotten. Any change might break the spell.

During the day they saw little of each other. Henry was out on his horse from early morning till dusk, riding round the farms, getting to know his tenants and employees, and seeing to every detail of the running of his estate himself. He was determined to make it a model of what a country estate should be, and was fast succeeding. He was a popular and respected landlord. Autocratic and demanding, impatient with fools, he was yet kind and strictly fair. He could be disarmed by an honest rogue but never fooled by him. Above all he was a sportsman and anyone who shared his tastes was his friend, regardless of his circumstances or station in life. The new game of cricket, originally started by villagers in Hampshire and Kent, was becoming popular with the gentry throughout the country and Henry was one of the first in Dorset to organise a team. This comprised members of his household, blacksmiths, farmworkers and neighbouring gentlemen. They met and played on his excellent ground with the utmost conviviality.

Sarah's day was spent almost entirely in the company of her mistress. In Anne's apartments, the nursery or the garden, she accompanied her on visits to the ladies of the neighbourhood. Bryanston was no isolated manor and Dorset was far from dull. Apart from Blandford, where there were some fine town houses, there were several estates which lay within five miles of Bryanston. Amongst them were the Seymers at Hanford; Henry's cousins the Ryves at Ranston, whose daughter had recently married his brother Edward Berkeley; the Bowers at Iwerne; and Anne's sister Meliora, now married to Squire Fownes of Stepleton. Mrs. Fownes was a constant visitor to Bryanston. Ten years older than her sister she was full of sage advice on the handling of husbands and children and on the management of the household of which she had once been mistress herself. Anne would listen politely but regarded it not at all. The sisters were different in every possible way but as Anne one day told Sarah, with an unexpected malicious glint in her eye, she did not think her dear sister could be so very clever for the story was that her husband Henry Portman had offered her the fine house he had built in Sherborne for her residence after his decease, this she had refused to accept on the grounds that it was no more than a hostelry, a resting place between the Dorset and Somerset estates. As a result the widowed Meliora had been left with no residence at all, for the Portman estates being entailed on the Berkeley's this was all old Henry had had to offer. Fortunately, Meliora had not long remained a widow and now appeared to be trying to make up for past and lost glories by making her new husband spend far more than he either wished, or could afford, on improvements to his house at Stepleton.

With Henry in residence they entertained more frequently at Bryanston and it was usually gentlemen who came to dine and play cards with their host. Anne was in the habit of retiring early and for this Sarah was thankful for it was only when her mistress was settled for the night that she could escape to her secret world. When Henry had speeded his last guest on his way home or left him to snore in happy oblivion over the green baize if the wine had circulated too freely, he would join her in the little Pavilion. Fortunately it was no rude shelter. It was comfortably and elegantly furnished as a bower for 'my lady'. It had been constructed for Meliora, according to her wishes, by her aged and doting spouse. She too no doubt had found it a pleasant retreat, and it is possible that this was not the first time it had served as a sanctuary for illicit lovers.

14   Sarah's secret

AS THE golden summer days flew past Sarah was happy as only a woman can be, who must make the most of every precious moment, knowing that her happiness might be but a brief interlude. The days were growing shorter when Henry told her that he could no longer delay his visit to London. He wished to get his business done and return before the winter weather made the roads dangerous and unpleasant for travellers.

Sarah's heart gave a jolt. So it was the end of the chapter. Nothing would ever be the same again. By the time he returned, the nagging little worry she had firmly ignored for some weeks past might be impossible to ignore any longer.

Resolutely she smiled at him. "Is it truly your intention to return so soon. Will you not find the pleasures of the town too tantalizing after your long sojourn in the country?"

"Horrid creature, do you doubt my constancy," he laughed, "you need not." Kissing her lightly he said "I will come back for this. And besides," he added teasingly, "I must return for my partridges."

Sarah nodded with mock seriousness.

"What an adle-pate I am, I should know you would not neglect them. What a strange fondness it is you have for those poor little birds, which you rear with such tender care only for the pleasure of killing them."

Henry was about to return some casual reply to this sally, when he noticed Sarah's expression. The smile had gone from her eyes and suddenly she looked sad and forlorn.

"Why you goose," he said at last. "Does that trouble you. It should not, my love. They have a short life but a happy one, I assure you." He took her in his arms and kissed her again, anxious to remove the hurt, lost look from her face.

Sarah's smile returned instantly, and as she wound her arms tightly round his neck there was a provocative gleam in her eyes.

"I am reassured entirely, kind sir, so now we need waste no more time discussing your favourite sport."

Henry in full agreement with this decision closed her mouth with a kiss and found her response more passionate than ever before. He was long to remember the sweetness and delight of their love-making that night.   Reluctant to part they stayed wrapped in each others arms until the stars visible through the windows began to fade and the first grey light of daybreak warned them that they must delay no longer if they were to seek their own apartments unseen by one or other of the servants whose day started before the sun was up.

Sarah stood over Melody's bed in a corner of the attic room which the girl shared with two young housemaids.   Wearing only a petticoat, with a shawl flung round her shoulders, she spoke in a whisper, shivering with cold.   "Melody, wake up—wake up, attend my lady for me this morning, tell her I am unwell.   And see if you need not be so clumsy as usual or she will surely send for me."   It took her some time and much shaking to arouse the girl who slept heavily, not surprisingly, for cold as it was, the small chamber with its one tiny sealed window under the eaves was close. What little fresh air could penetrate during the day had been used and vitiated by the sleeping women so that over all hung the stench of straw-filled mattresses, coarse woollen covers, and the stale smell of decades of serving maids.   If Melody did not soon respond she was sure to be sick again.

At last Melody sat up rubbing the sleep from her eyes.   "Why, what ails you Sarah?"

"'Tis nothing but a chill, if I keep to my bed until noon I shall be well enough."   With that she was gone and Melody was denied the pleasure of telling her how white and sickly she looked, and that in all likelihood it was the pox of which they would all surely die. Fortunately Melody was too busy all morning to spread her alarming and ill-founded opinion through the household and when Sarah appeared to resume her duties looking none the worse for her early indisposition, Melody was reluctantly forced to abandon it.

Later that afternoon Sarah went down to Durweston to see the Godwyns.   It was months since she had visited them although she had sometimes seen her Uncle Josiah at Bryanston.   He was a frequent visitor, for the steward was a good friend of his and they enjoyed a pipe and a gossip together, in the course of which many tankards of the Manor's home-brewed ale was consumed between them before they could in fairness decide whether it was superior or inferior to Josiah's at the Inn.

Before these sessions, he had sometimes sought her out but they rarely exchanged more than a few words for Sarah always made her escape before he could ask too many questions. Afterwards there was no necessity for her to avoid him for they finished late and Josiah only wished to be put upon his old mare who would carry him slowly but safely home. Sarah had written a note to Damon telling him that her Mistress, to whom she owed so much kindness, could not contemplate losing her that she herself was not yet ready to marry and he must forget her. When this was dispatched she had no choice but to avoid the Inn. Sorry as she was to lose touch with her relatives, the risk of seeing Damon was too great, and for his sake it was better that they should not meet. Nor could she face good Mrs. Godwyn's sympathy, advice and admonishments to look out for herself and marry whom she pleased, which she knew would be forthcoming. It was only the most urgent of reasons which finally forced her to go to the Inn, and she prayed that she would find her Aunt alone.

Her prayer was answered and Mrs. Godwyn welcomed her like a long lost daughter. Evidently she bore no resentment for Sarah's neglect and all the blame was to be put on poor Anne's slender shoulders.

"Well now, come you in and sit by the fire," she said after embracing Sarah warmly. "Tis a shame the way they keep you so close at the Manor, does her Ladyship work you so very hard? Though you look well enough, my love, and prettier than ever I declare!" She took Sarah's fur-trimmed bonnet and cloak and set them carefully on a chair.

"That would be one of her Ladyship's I expect," she went on, admiring the bonnet. "I am glad she sees to it that you are clad decent, with all she asks of you."

Sarah did not inform her that it was one that Henry had given her. Smuggled first to their rendezvous, and thence by Sarah to her bedroom it had remained hidden until today when she had dared to wear it.

"Now tell me your news, it was summer when you last was here," Aunt Loveday rattled on and proceeded to give almost a day to day account of all that had happened at the Inn during the past months, while Sarah warmed her hands at the leaping log fire, appearing to listen attentively though her thoughts were elsewhere.

"Squire Fownes of Stepleton was here but a month ago, with his lady. Own sister she is I believe to the lady Anne, and was once Mistress of Bryanston too, so I am told. There's an odd circumstance. On their way home from Bath they were held up by one of these rapscallions on the road, no more than a mile or so back.

That is why they stopped here. The poor lady was distraught, and near to hysterics, after her horrid experience. Though I doubt the rascal took much from them. They say Mr. Fownes is close to bankruptcy, for he has spent so much on improving his house and more on breeding these fox-hounds, which they do say are the first in the country. 'Tis foolish waste if the money's not to spare, and so his lady thinks, I understand, for I could not help but overhear her complaints whilst they rested right here in the parlour for an hour, and took some refreshment."

As if reminded by her last remark, Mrs. Godwyn set about laying a snowy white cloth on the table, and setting various articles from a well-stocked cupboard upon it, not for a moment ceasing her monologue.

"There now, and did I not tell you that we were honoured by a visit from your Master, the Squire of Bryanston himself?" Sarah looked up, then quickly away into the fire, but now she was listening. "No indeed, I could not have done, I remember well 'twas the very next day after you was here, for Josiah made mention that you were his niece, and the young Squire was pleased to speak kindly of you. He had ridden up from his estates in Somerset, and in the shortest time of which ever I heard." Her broad face wreathed in smiles, she continued to address the back of Sarah's head.

"Ah, Sarah, there's a fine young gentleman," she went on. "T'would take more than one rascally highwayman to stop him on the road, I'll warrant, and if there were more I doubt they'd catch him if he chose to gallop on."

"Aunt Loveday . . ." desperately Sarah attempted to halt the flow but with little success.

"There my dear, how I do run on and you must be starved. Wait whilst I call that idle wench. There was a bird ready dressed and should be done by now."

Mrs. Godwyn bustled out of the room and returned shortly bearing a large platter on which rested, in all its golden succulent glory, a plump young fowl roasted to a turn.

"Come Sarah, sit to the table, love, if I must talk, and I own 'tis a fault I cannot cure, at least you shall eat."

Again Sarah tried to speak but at that moment the maidservant entered bearing more smoking dishes which she set upon the already loaded table. There was nothing for it but to allow herself to be conducted by her kindly aunt towards it, although not one morsel of its delicious burden did she have the least desire to sample.

"Now, as I was saying," Mrs. Godwyn went on, as she neatly carved the bird, "as handsome a gentleman as ever I saw, with a sweet disposition and a kindly humour, and so I've been told before, but 'twas the first time I'd the opportunity to judge for myself and indeed am convinced 'tis nothing but the truth. You are fortunate Sarah, to serve in the house of a gentleman of such quality. There are upstarts enough, as we all know, without a notion how to treat their dependants and servants." She sighed and glanced at the little maid who still hovered around the table. "Now get along Jenny, there's work to be done in the dairy. We have no more need of you here." As the door closed behind the girl, she placed a heaped platter in front of Sarah. "I was about to say, my dear, that if you are indeed resolved not to accept poor Damon, for so Josiah tells me, it is a comfort to know you are so well placed at the Manor."

Sarah pushed the food away from her and rose abruptly to her feet.

"Aunt Loveday," she said, "I must speak to you. Please listen to me." She turned and walked towards the fire, having at last silenced her aunt who now regarded her with open-mouthed surprise, and then cast a regretful glance at the good food lying abandoned on the table.

"You may hate me and despise me if you will, but I beg of you to help me." She paused and stood gazing into the fire as if seeking help from the blazing logs. Before Mrs. Godwyn could find her voice, however, Sarah turned and faced her across the little parlour. Softly and clearly she said, "I am going to have a child."

For a moment Mrs. Godwyn could make no sense of this quietly spoken statement. Sarah stood straight and still, her head held high, her eyes clear and wide caught and held her aunt's. Mrs. Godwyn was the first to lower her own. Her merry face crumpled with perplexity. Here was no suppliant, no shame-faced miss, no cringing or crying, no excuses or accusations, which commonly went with such an admission. Only a cold proud desperation in the eyes, which had held her own. Feeling strangely uncomfortable, it was some moments before Mrs. Goldwyn could gather her thoughts, but at last, aided by a shrill whistle and the clanking of pails from across the yard which broke the singing silence which had fallen between them, she recovered. Leaving the table she approached her niece.

"There now Sarah, what a sly one you are, and I'd thought it was all over between you, but why distress yourself, you silly child.

Damon will be overjoyed, for now you must marry without delay, and your lady cannot prevent you. Never fear, you be by no means the first to ask Parson's blessing a trifle late in the day, and where's the harm in it? 'Tis usual practice hereabouts. Ay, but you've kept your secret well my love, and Damon too, not one word has he let drop, though we have seen little enough of him since you've not been visiting here. Always up to Bryanston he was this last summer, playing a new fangled game of the Squire's, or so I was told. But there, my dear, you'll know all about that and now I know what kept him away, and it wasn't the ale and the company in the Steward's room after all," she said with a broad smile. Then with an appraising glance at the girl's slim figure, she added, "Ay, a fine couple you'll make, but we must hasten the ceremony before there's an alteration in your shape."

Gently, Sarah removed Mrs. Godwyn's plump hand which rested on her shoulder. She dreaded dealing her a further and far worse blow but the longer her aunt was allowed to delude herself the more difficult it would be and the harder it would fall.

"Aunt Loveday," she said firmly, "Please understand, I need your help, not your congratulations. I will not, indeed I cannot, marry Damon." Quickly she placed a finger on her aunt's lips as that indefatigable body opened her mouth to speak once more. "He is not the father of my child." Sarah added, "Nor have I set eyes on him since the day I was last here in your house."

This not only effectively silenced the poor woman but caused her to collapse in astonished dismay into the nearest chair. Whilst she had the chance Sarah went on.

"Forgive me, dear Aunt, but I have no intention of disclosing the name of my lover. If for this reason you refuse to help or advise me you must say so, and I must seek help elsewhere. Above all I am resolved for the sake of my child that my shame shall not be known in this neighbourhood. If you will not give me your aid I must entreat you to guard my confidence even if in your heart you condemn my incontinence."

In a strangled voice, Mrs. Godwyn managed to say, "But Sarah, this fellow must marry you."

"That is impossible," Sarah replied, with an odd little smile, "the 'fellow' is already married."

15   Questions in the house

HENRY HAD been in a vile mood for days, coldly sarcastic to his wife, peremptory to the servants and indifferent even to the fawning of his favourite dog.   It was so unlike him to be thus, that everyone in the house was on tenterhooks lest they say or do the wrong thing. Even Laetitia, who had lately returned from Bath, guarded her tongue after one unfortunate remark, which Henry would normally have ignored, aroused him to such a passion that for once she feared the consequences of her impertinence.

He had returned from London in his usual good spirits having transacted that business which months ago he had informed his wife was so urgent.   It seemed not to have suffered from his long delay in attending to it.   His return home, within fourteen days, had surprised Anne who had been convinced that once he became involved with his gambling friends in Town even his favourite pursuits of shooting and hunting would not entice him back to the country for many weeks.

His ill-humour did not become apparent until a few days after his return.   Sarah was the cause of it.   Having finished his business as expeditiously as possible, he had set off for Dorset again.   He was deaf to the persuasions of his friends and scarcely admitted even to himself the reason for his anxiety to return.   Leaving London at dawn and riding post he had covered the hundred odd miles to Bryanston in one day.   It was late when he arrived and he had retired to bed immediately.   The next day he found no opportunity for a word alone with Sarah but sure that she would be awaiting him at the summerhouse he repaired there at the usual time.   When she did not come, disappointed as he was, he was not apprehensive and only determined to make a definite arrangement with her on the morrow.   Sarah, however, proved to be elusive and he found it impossible to get a word alone with her.   After three days with no success he was forced to pen a note which he hoped to smuggle into her hand.   He was thoughtful as he carefully trimmed a quill. "Minx, so it seems we must court her.   And so we shall," he said aloud, as he set ink to paper.

The note, however, proved unnecessary.   As he was leaving the library where he had so carefully penned it he ran straight into Sarah going towards the stair leading to her Mistress's apartments.

For a moment he could not be sure it was her, for the corridor was ill-lit and with face averted she would have hurried past him without so much as a glance if he had not firmly caught her arm and swung her round to face him. Without a word he drew her back into the library and closed the door behind them. He regarded her quizzically, there was no reproach in his manner, relieved only to have contacted her at last, he was more amused than annoyed by her avoidance of him.

"La, ma'am," he said at last, "must I woo you all over again, and after such a short absence. You must know I did not delay my return a day longer than was necessary."

Sarah made no reply, she was pale and her eyes, yellow as a cat's, stared up at him with as little expression.

Henry felt in his pocket for the neatly folded missive he had so recently completed, and held it out to her.

"Will this not soften your heart, my love? I confess the writing of such letters is not my greatest accomplishment, indeed I cannot remember an occasion when I have found it necessary to exercise it. You must therefore forgive my lack of style and regard only the sincerity of the sentiments it contains."

Taking her in his arms he added, "You may, however, read it later at your leisure if you wish, for I know a far better way of expressing them." He kissed her gently at first and then more urgently, for though she was unresisting in his embrace he felt an aloofness in her which had never before come between them. With it, a disturbing flicker of doubt and anxiety stirred in his mind.

Aloud he said, "You will meet me tonight? Give me your word."

When she did not immediately reply, he held her at arms length and gently shook her. "Speak Sarah, what game is this, do you think to tease me for ever?"

Sarah shook her head and spoke for the first time since she had entered the room.

"I will be at the Folly tonight, but you must know it will be for the last time."

"What nonsense is this?"

"Please," Sarah broke in, "We cannot talk here but it is true—'tis all finished. I must go now before I am missed," and slipping quickly by him she reached the door and was gone in a moment. Henry was too surprised to prevent her leaving.

Puzzled and uneasy, he paced the floor and stared unseeingly at the books which lined the walls. One thing of which he had

become quite certain during this summer was that however lightly
he might himself regard their liaison, Sarah loved him.   He had
been surprised at her easy surrender at first, but had not long
remained in any doubt as to her true feelings.   Sarah was no
wanton, and he could not believe that during his short absence she
could have fallen victim to some other man's charms.   He pulled a
book from the shelf and flipped over the pages, frowning over the
small print without reading a single word.

"Then why the devil should she want to end it," he shouted
suddenly, flinging the book down on the table.

The moon was almost full and it was a bright cold night.   Sarah
kept to the shadows of the tall yew hedges as she made her way
through the gardens towards their rendezvous.   She was early and
though she did not expect that Henry would join her for some time
she was content to be alone for a while.   As she approached the
little building, however, she could see that the lantern which provided not only light but a little warmth on cold nights, was already
lit.   So he was there already, waiting.   A wild rush of love for him
surged up in her, and she stayed still for a moment her hand on her
fast beating heart.   Every instinct in her urged to run to him.
Forget her carefully rehearsed story of why she was forced to leave
Bryanston, and with his arms about her, forget and ignore for just a
few more weeks the predicament she was in.

It was as she stood there still undecided that the head and shoulders of someone inside appeared for a moment outlined against the
warm glow of the lighted window.   Sarah went cold.   It was not
Henry.   Cloaked and hooded, shapeless and anonymous, it was,
nevertheless, a woman.   Anne?   Had she discovered their secret?
Panic-stricken, for a moment Sarah wanted to fly, run away, anywhere.   Then she realised with relief that whoever it was it could
not possibly be her mistress, for she herself had only stopped to
fetch a cloak before leaving the house after helping Anne to undress
and seeing her settled for the night.   Then who could it be?   Sarah
moved nearer, until she was just below the lighted window, where
she stood wondering what to do.   Should she wait here for Henry
or return and try to intercept him.   It might well be another hour
before he came.   Before she could make up her mind she caught the
murmur of voices and realised that there was more than one inter-
loper.   Holding her breath, she listened, every nerve taut, hoping
to get some clue as to their identity.   Then quite clearly she heard a

woman's high, affected laugh as the door, at the top of the steps not
ten paces from her, opened. It was followed by a man's quiet slow
drawl, the words were not clear but the voice was unmistakeable.
It was Henry's.

This time Sarah obeyed her impulse to run. Without stopping to
think or consider she fled down the grass path, repeating sound-
lessly, over and over again, the one word "No, no, no."

On reaching her own small bedchamber she flung herself on the
low pallet and gave way to a fit of passionate sobbing. It was the
culmination of weeks of silent despair and suppressed worry.
Even at the interview with her aunt she had not for a moment lost
her self-control. At the end of it she had thanked her for the
promised help, and coolly agreed that the proposed plan which the
good woman had conceived when she could at last collect her wits,
was excellent; but she had neither discussed her feelings nor asked
or accepted sympathy from her. For her child's sake she had
needed help in this situation to which her own wickedness had
brought her, and Mrs. Godwyn had not failed her. Sarah was
prepared to go away and renounce her lover, that would be punishment enough, she had thought bitterly, but she had no intention of
telling Henry of her plight or allowing anyone to know the part he
had played in it. Now for the second time he had returned sooner
than she had thought possible. Once more to break her resolve
never to see him again and with disastrous consequences. For the
events of this night convinced her that Henry regarded her so little
that at the first hint of her intention to part from him, he had
wasted no time in finding consolation, and could even contemplate
an assignation with another in their own secret meeting place. In
her unhappy and emotional state of mind Sarah felt as if her heart
would break and she did not stop to consider for one moment that
there could be any other explanation.

Henry escorted Laetitia back through the moonlit garden to the
house. To his surprise and annoyance he had found her in the
summer-house on his arrival. He did not believe her explanation
that she had had gone for a walk in the cool night air to clear a
headache. He was sure that either she had arranged to meet
someone in the Folly, or, more probably, had discovered some
reason to suspect that he himself used the place for this purpose.
Laetitia, being Laetitia, had determined to find out.

If this were so, Henry did not intend that her curiosity should be
satisfied. Impatient as he was to remove her from the scene, he
showed no sign of it. Hoping that if Sarah arrived she would hear

their voices and remain concealed without, he calmly kept Laetitia
in conversation, until he could, without appearing to hurry her,
suggest that they returned to the house. As they walked slowly
back, they were both silent. Henry still did not know the true
reason for Laetitia's presence, nor had he deigned to give her any
explanation of his own, but of one thing he was sure—although he
had every intention of returning to meet Sarah later that night the
Folly would no longer be a safe rendezvous, and other arrangements
would have to be made. It now occurred to him that perhaps this
was the reason why Sarah had avoided it and of her unexpected
statement that she would meet him no more after tonight. Possibly
in his absence she had found out that Laetitia had discovered their
retreat. Silly child, he smiled to himself, did she really suppose
that this would prove an insurmountable obstacle?

His moodiness and irritability started the next day when he
learnt that Sarah had gone from Bryanston. Henry first heard it
casually from a servant and he went directly to his wife's boudoir to
discover the reason, wondering how he could bring the matter up
and question her without showing his concern. He need not have
worried, for Anne could speak of nothing else. Plaintively she told
him all and more than he wanted to know, of how Sarah had
behaved oddly of late, how she had neglected her duties, sent
Melody to attend her on several occasions, how forgetful and dis-
trait she had been these last weeks whilst he was in London.

"'Tis my firm belief," said Anne, "that she has a lover. The
cloddish farmer's boy, no doubt, whom she wished to marry some
time ago. I protest Sir," she went on, "I cannot understand the
child, why should she wish to throw herself away. Sarah may have
no fortune but she is a gentlewoman. I assured her that if she
would only not be in such haste to marry and would stay with me a
year or so longer, an excellent match might have been arranged for
her. Indeed I ventured to add, I felt sure that you, Sir, would not
be ungenerous and might well give her a portion when the time
came."

Henry bowed and in a voice as coolly indifferent as he could
make it ventured at last to interrupt and ask a question.

"Did she give no explanation; no warning? Am I to understand
Ma'am, she has left here today without a word?"

Anne shook her head.

"Melody brought this to me this morning." She picked up a
sheet of paper closely covered with Sarah's neat round writing.
"You will not wish to give yourself the trouble of reading it Sir,

and I am convinced there is not a word of truth in't."

Henry, however, took it from her, and moving towards the window read the note carefully.

> *Bryanston.*
> *2nd October, 1739.*
>
> *Dear Madam,*
> *I must beg your forgiveness for the great inconvenience my departure will cause you. I did warn you a week past that my Aunt Godwyn was in distress about her daughter in Poole and begged me to visit her and stay at her side until her husband's return from his voyage. God knows when that will be but in the meanwhile she needs me. This morning I received an Urgent Summons.*
> *Forgive me, dear Madam.*
> *I remain your obedient, humble servant,*
> *Sarah Godwyn*

The note revealed nothing of Sarah's emotional disturbance when she wrote it but nor did it ring true. As he read it Henry found his disbelief in Anne's theory that Damon was the real reason for Sarah's departure slowly giving way to an angry conviction that she was right. He tossed the letter carelessly down on the table and without comment took his departure, leaving Anne still bemoaning Sarah's inexplicable behaviour.

16   Followed to Poole

THE CREAKING of the Inn sign swinging gently on its chains attracted his attention. Henry pulled up his horse and regarded it thoughtfully. It depicted a white painted five barred gate, straddling a road which wound upwards towards unbelievably bright green hills outlined against a hard blue sky. Henry had no intention of calling at the Inn when he set out. Durweston belonged to the Cokes. They took little interest in and seldom visited this small parcel of land which did not even boast a manor house and was far distant from their extensive estates in Norfolk. For this reason Henry was hopeful that one day he might be able to acquire it.

Its sporting possibilities were excellent and marching as it did with Bryanston it would improve and round off his property. However, he found himself drawn there as if by a magnet after a tour of this neighbouring property. This was not the first time he had made a tour of inspection, riding up the valleys and over the downland from where he could see away to Poole Harbour on the south and Wyn Green, the highest point in Wiltshire, to the north. Always he finished up down in the village where this highly painted Inn sign seemed to merit more of his attention than all the rest of the cottages and buildings put together. Today, however, for the first time he dismounted and tossing the reins and a silver coin to a delighted small boy, he strode into the house.

During the winter Henry had spent very little time in Dorset Only so long as there were partridges to be shot had he remained at Bryanston and in the pursuit of sport he was able to put Sarah out of his mind if not out of his heart, although he did not acknowledge that she still had a place there. Incredulous and angry as he had been at first by her desertion, when no further word came from her he began to believe that he had been completely deceived in his judgment of her character and refused to admit how painfully he felt her loss.

From Anne, he did not expect, nor would he seek, comfort. He had come to realise very soon that nothing he could do would change this strange ice-maiden whom he had married, into the loving indulgent mate he had once visualised. If there had been any hope of it his affair with Sarah might not have become so important to him. Any idea of turning to his wife now and forcing his attentions upon her was abhorrent to him. Anne had played her part and would continue to do so as Mistress of Bryanston, a role that she filled to perfection now that she had lost, to a great extent, her shyness and nervousness in company. She was beautiful, gracious and universally admired both for her looks and her accomplishments. She had given him a son, she was his wife—that was unalterable but Henry no longer had any wish to win her love or insist that she continue to be his wife in anything more than name.

Estate business had taken him to Somerset, and again to London, in spite of the hazards of the roads which indeed served him excellently as an excuse, if excuse were needed, to remain in Town and to more or less resume his bachelor life. The convivial company in "White's" of which he had been a popular member since he came of age, had helped to pass the time tolerably well, but London life seemed to have lost its savour. High gambling was no longer so exciting as in earlier days when the turn of a card could mean near ruin or the thrill of short-lived wealth, and as for the pretty bawds and ladies of quality, if of doubtful virtue, of whom there was as wide a choice as ever in the Metropolis, he found them all a dead bore after a very short while. When he returned to Bryanston in the spring he was happy enough to be home again.

Sarah, however, was still absent and short of direct questioning he could discover no news of her whereabouts. Firmly he assured himself that it was mere idle curiosity as to what had become of her which finally took him into the Inn at Durweston.

Mistress Godwyn was evasive and quite unlike her usual loquacious self. Bustling about, ordering the maids to bring refreshment, to mend the fire in the best parlour, attending to all his comforts, she seemed however reluctant to stay and gossip which was all the Henry wanted though he could hardly express this wish to her. At last he had to resort to a direct question.

"And your niece Mistress, the pretty Sarah, she is well?"

Mrs. Goldwyn bumbled around the room nervously, like a monstrous bee trapped on the inside of a window pane.

"Your Honour is very kind to enquire, she does well, I thank you."

Henry waved his hand towards a chair.

"Pray be seated Ma'am, it makes me devilish uncomfortable to see you so busy."

Mrs. Godwyn seated herself reluctantly on the very edge of the chair Henry had indicated and regarded him mutely.

Half an hour later Henry took his leave. He had learnt very little, Mrs. Godwyn had willingly volunteered information about everything and everyone except her niece and the few facts he had managed to glean about her served only to deepen the mystery of Sarah's sudden departure from Bryanston.

As he rode slowly home Henry thought over what he had heard. Damon Hardy could have had nothing to do with it after all. He was in fact shortly to marry a neighbouring farmer's daughter. He gathered only that Sarah was in Poole looking after the Godwyn's daughter-in-law, just as she had said in her note to Anne. But why? Henry was perfectly well aware that Sarah had never set eyes on any member of Josiah's family until she came to Bryanston. Why should she leave Anne whom she had served for so long, to go and nurse a stranger. Why leave without a word of explanation to himself? She had loved him, they had been happy. What had happened in those two short weeks of his absence in London to cause her so suddenly to change? Conscience? Remorse? No, Henry did not believe it for one moment. Sarah's rigid puritanical upbringing had not altered her essential character. She would admit her sins and be prepared to accept punishment if it came, but she was no 'holier than thou' bigot who would race to meet it.

Suddenly Henry jerked at the reins and came to a standstill. "Accept her punishment!" Oh God, what a blind fool he had been! Suddenly all was clear, including Sarah's odd mood and abandoned love-making the night before he left for London, as if she knew it was to be their last. Her eyes that day in the libary after his return, wide and blank in her pale face, with a hint of despair in them which he had not then had the sense to recognise. And Mrs. Godwyn's kindly face puckered with worry and embarrassment today whenever Sarah's name was mentioned.

Henry dug his heels into his horse's flanks and urged him into a canter. He rode into the stable yard, called his groom and ordered him to saddle a fresh horse. He would be leaving immediately for Poole.

17   Forcing the issue

IT WAS dark when Henry arrived in Poole. He made his way directly to the quay where he demanded of a passerby where he could find a decent hostelry. On being informed that there was a fair house not one hundred yards along the quayside, Henry then asked if by any chance he had knowledge of the whereabouts of the house of a Master Godwyn.

"Why, you be in luck Sir," replied his informant, "For if 'tis Captain Godwyn you want his house lies cheek by jowl against 'The Anchor', the very Inn to which I have this minute directed your Lordship."

Thanking him, Henry rode on.

There was a lantern over the door of the Inn, and more light came from the uncurtained windows on either side, throwing broad yellow bands onto the cobbled quayside. The place look neat and clean enough. Huddled against it, as if seeking protection from its larger neighbour, was a small timbered house. This must undoubtedly be Captain Godwyn's. The stranger's description was certainly apt. Here too an upper window was brightly lit. As Henry slowly dismounted, his eyes still on the window, the landlord of the Inn appeared.

Henry returned his polite greeting absentmindedly and then recovered himself sufficiently to inform his host that he would require his best bedchamber for the night, a dining parlour, if such were available, and that above all his horse should be attended to properly and put into a clean stable which he would himself inspect later. A boy appeared at the horse's head and led him away while the landlord bowed low and assured his 'lordship' that both his own and his horse's needs could be met more than adequately, and if his lordship would but step inside he would see for himself what superior comforts "The Anchor" had to offer, "For did it not cater for Quality of the highest rank." There was not a chamber in the house that he would be ashamed to offer to a belted Earl! Henry cut him short, though he made no move to enter mine host's hospitable door.

"I will dine within the hour," he said. "In the meanwhile I will take your word for the comforts of which you boast. In truth I expect little and require only that my bedchamber be clean and the food edible. If you will kindly see to it, I will join you later for I have a call to make on your neighbour, Captain Godwyn. Am I correct in assuming that this is his house?" Henry added, nodding towards the lighted casement which his eyes had hardly left for a moment.

"Indeed to be sure, you are right Sir, but if your lordship will forgive the impertinence, I would dare to suggest that if your business is not urgent you will let it wait until the morning." The landlord flinched as Henry glared at him, but continued bravely, "'Tis Mistress Godwyn, Sir. She is confined and has been in labour since noon today. There is still no news that her child is safely delivered. My good wife would be the first to know, vexed though she be that she has not been asked to assist. Ten of her own she's brought into the world, and six of 'em living," he added proudly. "Many's the neighbour who has been glad of Betsy's help, for she knows what she's about does Betsy. But they be queer folk. Quakers they do say. Keep to themselves they do."

Henry glanced up once more at the window, but he did not attempt this time to interrupt. The landlord had followed his glance and shaking his head mournfully went on, "'Tis not surprising the poor young woman should have a difficult confinement, ten years married and this the first." Henry raised his eyebrows and looked interested.

"Ah, now I understand your concern. You are entirely right landlord, and a man of sensibility I perceive. Let us go in and sample the excellence of your hostelry. My business with Godwyn can well wait until the morrow, when I sincerely trust your good wife will have better news of Mistress Godwyn."

The landlord led him into a small parlour where a fire of sea coal burned brightly in the polished grate, and assured him that here he would not be disturbed.

"There is meat and poultry ready dressed Sir, and you may dine whenever you wish, though perhaps first you will take a glass of wine. I think your lordship will not find our French wines at all inferior."

Henry smiled.

"I'll take that risk, and I do not doubt that you could also produce a passable brandy. When I have dined perhaps I may risk that too, and ask no questions as to how you came by it."

The landlord's face split into a huge grin.

"Your lordship is a gentleman after my own heart. Rest assured Sir, you will not be disappointed."

Henry spent an uneasy night, though it was through no fault of the Inn. His bed was toleraby comfortable and the linen coarse but clean. His dinner had been good and the wine and the brandy excellent. Nevertheless these material comforts did little to keep his mind from the house next door and Sarah's part in the drama that was taking place there. Having little doubt that the guess which had brought him here was correct, his concern for her made sleep impossible.

In the morning when he descended to the parlour he found the landlord's wife a willing informant. Expressing the hope that he had passed a restful night she went on to tell him that Mistress Godwyn was safely delivered and he need no longer delay his call on Master Godwyn.

"Though I know not whether the child be male or female or if the poor woman does well or no, for not one soul has been into or out of the house."

"Then why are you so sure 'tis all over," Henry asked.

"Why, bless you Sir, I heard the baby cry round four of the clock this morning. It sounded lusty enough, I trust its mother is equally well. Poor thing, confined to the house as she has been and scarce set foot out of doors these last months. She should have been tended by a body with experience. What good that chit of a girl could be to her I declare I do not know."

Henry successfully hid his relief at her news and demanded some breakfast. At this moment the landlord entered the room and chiding his wife for keeping the gentleman waiting with her woman's talk which could not possibly interest their guest, sent her off to get him something to eat.

Henry curbed his impatience as long as possible. He realised that it was not going to be easy to see Sarah, she was evidently well-guarded by her friends, but he was determined not to leave Poole without doing so. He did not hurry over his meal and afterwards strolled round to the stables to look at his horse, before finally knocking on the door of the little house next to the Inn. It was immediately opened by a broad shouldered, youngish man, with the unmistakeable stamp of the sea on him and Josiah Godwyn's clear blue eyes. He regarded his unexpected visitor with some surprise.

"Have I the pleasure of addressing Captain Godwyn?" Henry asked politely.

"Your servant Sir," the man bowed, but did not invite him to enter.

"I would be obliged if I might have a private word with you on a matter of some importance to . . . to both of us I think," Henry said taking a step forward.

Captain Godwyn hesitated for a moment and then with a shrug led the way into a small parlour. Unlike his neighbour there was no subservience in his bearing. As Henry followed, he took note of his surroundings. Inside the room he stayed near the door.

"My name is Henry Portman of Bryanston. I am well acquainted with your father who is a neighbour of mine. I desire to see your kinswoman, Sarah Godwyn. I understand she resides here with you."

"That is quite impossible." Godwyn's startled expression and immediate denial of his visitor's request left Henry in no further doubt as to the situation.

"May I ask why not?" he replied calmly.

"My wife," he hesitated, "She is indisposed. Sarah is with her, she cannot possibly leave her. Now if you will forgive me Sir, I must request you to go."

Henry judged that Captain Godwyn was not a practised liar. Though feeling sorry for the man, in his uncomfortable situation, he yet had to persist.

"I am afraid I must insist, although I regret this intrusion, for I understand that a child was born here only this morning?"

"That is no concern of yours," Godwyn replied hastily.

"I think I am the best judge of that, it may be that it is very much my concern." As he spoke Henry opened the door. "In the mean-while I must insist on seeing Sarah, will you conduct me to her or must I find my own way?"

Captain Godwyn moved fast. It was quite clear that he was a man of action not words, and evident that he was prepared to use force to prevent this unwelcome visitor from seeking out his cousin. Henry, however, was ready for him. His casual stance was deceiving and young Godwyn ran right on to the neat upper-cut which Henry delivered, regretfully, to the point of the gallant Captain's jaw, sending him reeling back across the room. Deciding that there would be a better time than the present to apologise for so vilely abusing his hospitality, Henry was out of the door and up the short wooden stair which he had carefully located earlier, before Tom Godwyn had recovered from this unexpected blow. On the dark little landing above he ducked just in time to avoid cracking his own head on a beam and ignoring an angry yell from below, he hesistated for only a moment before the two doors which confronted him. The murmur of women's voices decided him and he knocked on the door from behind which the sounds had come. Without waiting for an invitation, he opened the door and went in.

The room was low-ceilinged and dim, only a little sunlight filtered in through the casement before which a plump motherly figure stood holding in her arms a shapeless bundle in such tender fashion that it could only be a new born infant.

As he entered the woman's expression changed to one of astonishment and alarm and then her eyes went swiftly to the bed which almost filled the small room.

Henry followed her glance, and then stepping aside and holding open the door he said, with a slight bow, "Mistress Godwyn, be good enough to leave us, I must speak with your cousin alone."

Before the woman could protest a soft voice from the bed bade her do as she was asked. Without a word, clutching the babe to her, the woman dropped a curtsey and with downcast eyes hurried past Henry and out of the room. Quietly, he closed the door after her, and stepped closer to the bed. Sarah gazed up at him. Her eyes were misty green, yellow flecked in her pale face, her hair tumbled on the pillow was like a flame in the gloomy little room.

As Henry looked down at her he knew at last what had driven him so impetuously to this strange meeting at Sarah's bedside. It was not only a desire to help her in a predicament of which he himself was the cause. For almost the first time in his life he was at a loss for words, and discovering in himself feelings he had never before experienced. To enjoy life, to please himself, and others too, so long as it coincided with his own pleasure, to accept lightly the affection of friends, and the 'love' of women without involving his deepest emotions. That was the extent of his previous experience. Suddenly everything had changed. There was only one thing he wanted to say to Sarah at this moment, but the words he had spoken so often and so lightly, he could not speak now, instead, sitting down on the edge of the bed, he asked a question.

"Is it a boy?"

Sarah's eyes had never left his, she nodded then turned her head restlessly on the pillow in a soft expressionless voice, "He is not thy son, Berkeley."

For a moment Henry's face hardened, his hands clenched and then slowly relaxed. He reached out and very gently turned her head until once more she had to look into his eyes.

"Whose then?" he asked softly.

"Mine, only mine. I will take him to the church to be baptised and they will write his name in the parish register and after it will be written 'Sarah Godwyn, her bastard'." As she pronounced the word which gave her so much pain, Henry leant over and kissed her mouth.

"Does that matter so much my love," he said, "You know he is my son, now I know and swear I will never forget it. Why did you run away? Why did you not trust me?"

"What else could I do? Would you have had me stay to be reviled, despised and my son to be hurt and mocked; called that name? No, it was impossible. In loving you I thought to hurt no-one but myself. My sin seemed a little thing until I knew that our child might suffer for it."

"He will not, I swear it. If you wish I will acknowledge him. It has been done before and no-one will dare to say a word, if only you will come back to Bryanston."

"And Anne, your wife?" Sarah asked.

"She would not care, why should she?"

Sarah shook her head and smiled through her tears.

"You are wrong Henry, so very wrong. Anne is happy now, happier than she ever thought to be. As Mistress of Bryanston and the mother of your son, she has all she ever wanted. Our secret has not hurt her, but to know of it would destroy her little world entirely. Loving you is something I cannot help, but no-one else shall suffer for it, nor will our son. My friends have been very good, our plans are made."

"What plans? Tell me," Henry interrupted sharply.

"Cousin Tom's ship sails for America within the sennight. My son and I go with him. There we will make a new life."

"Sarah," there was desperation in Henry's voice. "Do you imagine I will let you go so easily now that I have found you again." Gently he lifted her into his arms.

"No," she murmured, "'tis settled."

Henry held her closer, "I love you, Sarah, I love you and will not lose you now. These last months I have not known a moment's happiness." He kissed her gently. "Fool that I was knowing not what ailed me nor admitting the cause of my distemper, those around me have suffered too," he added ruefully. "Listen to me Sarah, everything shall be as you wish. We will guard our secret but I will think of a plan so that you may stay near me. No-one shall suffer for it, I swear it. You are the mother of my son, nothing can alter that and in my heart you will be my wife, if only it were possible . . ."

He stopped, arrested by the look in Sarah's eyes. Tired as they were, still blurred with tears, they had changed. The blank hurt look had gone, suddenly they shone with happiness. Her fingers caressed his cheek and for the first time she smiled, her mouth on his stopped him saying more.

Sarah felt as if she floated on a cloud. All the misery of the last months seemed to fall away leaving her body light and free, her mind emptied of the fears which had probed and taunted her daily. With Henry's arms round her she was safe again. Knowing that whatever the future held this moment would always be with her, she wanted only to sleep now; to stay a little longer in this dream world where Henry loved her, needed her and would not let her go away on a frightening voyage to an unknown land. Exhausted by the long hours in childbirth, followed by Henry's unexpected visit, Sarah was incapable of further argument or decision.

"I love you" she murmured. Her eyes were closed as Henry gently laid her back on the pillows. She was asleep. Henry touched her cheek, then quietly leaving the room descended to the parlour to make his peace with young Godwyn. As he entered Tom stepped towards him, white-faced and angry, his hands clenched aggressively.

"Mr. Portman, Sir," he started. Henry raised his hand.

"Please allow me to explain. You must find my conduct inexcusable; in any other circumstances indeed it would certainly have been so and I sincerely offer you my most humble apologies." Tom glared furiously at his unwelcome guest but could not find the words to express his indignation.

"As you are unlikely to accept them without a full explanation," Henry went on, "Be good enough to listen to me a minute or two. May I sit down?" For answer Tom strode to the door and flung it open.

"Pray leave my house immediately." Henry shrugged and ignored the demand. "Very well, I must be blunt. The child Sarah bore last night is my son. I am obliged to you, Sir, for sheltering her and concealing her dilemma from the world but it is no longer a secret from me."

Tom's open-mouthed expression of astonishment left Henry in no doubt that this information came as a complete surprise to him.

"So Sarah did not tell you?" he asked. Tom shook his head

dumbly. It was evident that he was quite out of his depth and could no longer cope with this situation. He made for the open door.

"I will send my wife to speak to you," he said and was gone.

Henry paced the small room nervously as he waited, hoping that Mrs. Godwyn would be more forthcoming. He had not long to wait and was not disappointed.

Jane Godwyn came into the room carrying a tray on which stood a bottle of wine and three glasses. She begged Henry to be seated as she set it carefully down on the table.

"I doubt we'll get Tom to join us, poor lad, he knows not whether he be on his head or his heels. I had hoped it would all have been over before he returned from his voyage, but the child was late and I have had to bully and coax him to play his part these last days. You will take a glass of wine with me Sir?"

"You are very kind ma'am, indeed I will." Taking the proffered glass, he added, "And will drink first, if I may, to a woman of remarkable resourcefulness and ingenuity."

"I thank you Sir. Aye, but 'twas fortunate Tom was home for a full month last summer, for when I let it be known that I was at last with child after ten years, the neighbours were counting on their fingers and doing sums in their heads. Fortunate too that I was the eldest of ten children and helped my mother bring her last two into the world. We had no need of a midwife."

"Nevertheless, it could not have been easy to keep up such a deception." Henry picked up his glass, the sunlight caught the dark wine and it glowed redly between them. His eyes were on it as he asked quietly, "What has Sarah told you, ma'am?"

"Very little and not the name of the father." Jane's eyes met his in a long straight look in which there was neither accusation nor question.

"Then shall we drink to my son." As he drained his glass, Henry was reminded of another occasion when he had drunkenly made Sarah drink with him, a toast to his unborn sons.

Jane sipped her wine and set down her glass. "I guessed of course from the moment Sarah asked me to leave you alone together this morning. Till then I had no idea, 'twas a shock you bursting in upon us at such a time." She shook her head reproachfully, "I own I was vexed till I had time to collect my wits." Henry took her hand, "My admiration for you, ma'am, grows every mintue, now I must crave your indulgence further to help me make plans for his and Sarah's future. First pray, tell me is it true that you were proposing to take them both on your husband's ship to America?''

That was Sarah's notion. When Tom arrived home and announced America was to be his destination on the next voyage, she begged him to take her. In the new country Sarah thought to keep the child as her own. Who there, she argued, would know that she was other than a widow and her child legitimate born. My plan was to bring him up here as ours, I knew I could persuade Tom to agree and Sarah was resigned to it until her time was near and she suddenly conceived this wild notion of going to America.'' She sighed, ''It was difficult, she could talk of nothing else and so excited at the prospect, what could poor Tom say? He is a kindly man and could not refuse her.''

''And you, Mistress Godwyn? You do not approve this plan, you have no wish to go?''

Jane smiled and shook her head. ''No, and have no intention of doing so. You must understand Sir, 'tis necessary to humour someone in Sarah's condition. I have sometimes accompanied my husband on a short voyage, but Tom's ship is no place for a baby, she'll soon come to understand that. No, they'll be well enough here with me, you need not worry Sir. What matter who the child calls Mother, for my part 'tis no favour I am doing. Lonesome it is with Tom away so much and no child of my own to keep me company. Why it has been a pleasure and joy to me to have Sarah here all these months. Not to mention the fun of deceiving the neighbours.'' Her eyes sparkled with amusement as she patted her stomach. ''A good thing it is that I be broad built, nobbut a small cushion did I need under my stays at any time.''

Henry laughed, delighted with this kindly sensible woman who could find humour in what must have been a very difficult situation. ''You are extraordinarily tolerant ma'am. Do you not feel some righteous anger against me even though you show no disapproval of Sarah?''

''Who am I to judge either of you Sir. At a time like this there is but one enemy to fight and that is the malice, spite and cruelty of our fellows. As for your part in this, I have reason to know of Sarah's pride and learned to understand her character. It is my belief that you knew nothing at all about this child and did not intentionally abandon her when she most needed you. That you were lovers is one thing and a matter entirely for your own conscience. However you would not find me so tolerant if I thought you had used her cruelly.''

Henry bowed to her across the table. ''I am grateful ma'am for your understanding, I would rather you were my friend than my enemy."

They talked for a while, Henry aware that this woman, wise and kind with a heart to match her intelligence, was still coolly assessing him, his character, his weaknesses and his intentions. Presently he rose saying, "I will leave you now ma'am, you must have a deal with which to occupy yourself. I have already taken up too much of your time, you may rest assured that I will return very shortly." He looked down at her thoughtfully, "I have a plan, the details of which I must think out. It may well strain even your tolerance, I hope not, for I shall need your co-operation."

"I make no promise, Sir. It is from Sarah that you must seek agreement to your plans."

The calm uncompromising answer pleased Henry. Here was a woman who did not meddle, a rare species indeed. As she led the way out of the room, Jane suddenly exclaimed, hand to mouth. "There, fool that I be, would you not care to see the child?"

Henry laughed and shook his head. "Any other woman would have thrust him under my nose long since. No, I am of the opinion that he will look like any other babe of a few hours old. Let us give Sarah the pleasure of showing off her son on my next visit. Who knows, it may help to persuade her to my plan. In the meanwhile I am well aware that he is in excellent hands and will not benefit in the least by meeting his father at this early stage in his life."

"As you wish," Jane replied, making to open the street door. Gently, Henry drew her back into the shadow of the little passage.

"'Tis early days for you to be seen showing out a guest, Mrs. Godwyn." He smiled as she darted further back from the door and then added seriously, "Pray ma'am, understand this. I came here not knowing what I should find, not even knowing my own heart. Now I have no doubts. I love Sarah, I would find it hard to live without her and have no intention of doing so."

With that he was gone, leaving Jane Godwyn as firm and staunch an ally as any he was ever likely to find.

Henry was thoughtful as he rode back to Bryanston. He had to find a way to install Sarah as near to him as possible. On reflection he realised that she was right, from every point of view it would be impossible for her to return to Bryanston, a house in Blandford town perhaps would serve.

Whatever arrangements he made would have to depend on and include Jane Godwyn who had declared herself happy to assume the role of mother to the child in the eyes of the world.

Thinking back on the events of the last twenty-four hours he marvelled at the kindness and practical help extended to Sarah by the whole Godwyn family. They had ingeniously protected her right through her pregnancy and confinement, could he now ask more of Jane? Sarah, he knew, would not abandon the child to her, nor did he wish her to. If he was to establish her near to him, then Jane must come too. How could she be persuaded to do so? Suddenly the solution presented itself to him. Jane had admitted that her life was lonely in Poole, would not a house near to Tom's parents and shared with Sarah be an improvement rather than a sacrifice. Better too for the child to be brought up in the countryside among friends than on the busy quayside. Henry had no doubts that the boy's welfare would concern her.

Only yesterday, riding across the water meadows towards the Inn, he had passed without giving it a thought what he now hoped might be the answer to his problem. It was one of several unimportant small properties which he had inherited with the larger estates and almost forgotten. A dwelling house and a few acres, uninhabited and in disrepair but in a charming situation on the edge of the village of Durweston.

18   Interlude

AT THIS point in my story I did not quite know how to continue, I put it aside and as time went by, despaired of finishing it. There was a good reason. For me everything had changed. Since Michael died I had begun to lose the incentive to write. Lacking the peaceful routine of the life we had led together in those last years; the comfort of his presence and his interest in the project, it was becoming increasingly more difficult.

It had started as a brief history of the family, then Sarah Godwin appeared in my manuscript and seemed to take over. [Did I invent her? I don't know?] She certainly had well established herself long before I discovered her in the Parish Register where her death was recorded in 1798.] Finally, I realised that if I was to complete the family history, I had to come out of my dream-world and get back to reality.

The first information we were given about the house we came to live in after the war was that it had once been a Dame School, run by two old ladies called Godwin. Later, I was to discover that there were many Godwins in the village in the nineteenth century. The churchyard was thick with their tombs, all descended from Benjamin who died aged 97 in 1841. It was his son, Henry, who enlarged the house after his father's death, and the family remained there until the last member, a 90-year-old spinster daughter died in 1935. The long lease, on which the Godwin's had had it from the estate, had long since expired and the house came back into the possession of the Portmans.

When my father-in-law offered it to us after the war, we were prepared to accept it gratefully, sight unseen. Having lived in various furnished houses for the duration, we found ourselves virtually homeless. We had no wish to return to London and with four children, two dogs, a pregnant cat and sundry white mice and guinea pigs to house, we needed, not only a roof over our heads, but also a reasonable amount of space below it and a garden around it.

Portman Lodge provided all this more than adequately though dear old Uncle Seymour living in solitary state with a companion and a small army of servants at the dower house, pronounced it 'very small' and wondered sadly, 'how we would manage?' He would not have understood if I had told him that to us it was a palace. After our tiny flat in London and the ropy furnished cottages we had occupied during the war, it was unbelieveably spacious. So I smiled bravely and assured him we would try to fit ourselves in.

It was in September 1945 when we came to live in Durweston, Michael and I, our two children and his two children from his first marriage. The house was square, white painted, blue shuttered, solid, comfortable. It stood alongside the road with its back to the village facing south-eastwards over water meadows and parkland to the river. The valley view was beautiful, framed by the steep wooded cliff leading up to Bryanston on the west bank and by the rose-red barns and outbuildings of France farm lying snugly on the gentle slope of the hillside on the east bank of the river.

I fell in love with it at once. The house; it had attics and a cellar! The garden, high walled at the back against intrusion from the village; in front a wide lawn with two glorious cedar trees perfectly placed in the far corner. Only one blot, a magnificent Monkey Puzzle tree right opposite the front door, darkening our bedroom window, generally obstructing the view and a prickly person of whom we felt we could never make a friend. We had that down at once. Then the village, its rooftops visible over the garden wall. Not a house that matched its neighbour except for one terrace of seven charming Georgian cottages. There were brick, flint, cob and white washed walls, tiled roofs and slate roofs; gabled Victorian dwellings in neat pairs with ancient thatched cottages smothered with flowers squatting beside them, looking as though they too had grown out of the ground. A formless pattern to surprise and delight the eye bordering the village street as it winds up the hill to the church, whose Norman tower dominates the scene as it has done for six hundred years.

I fell in love with it and knew that this was where I wanted to put down my roots.

Roots were something I felt I desperately needed. Some people are born with them, others acquire them later or don't ever appear to need them, I did. My mother's were far away in the western mountains and fiords of Norway of which she often talked, delighting her children and grandchildren with tales of her childhood in that beautiful country. Of my father's Kentish background, I knew little for he was killed in the first war when I was too young to remember him. Born and brought up by a widowed mother who was not English, in the anonymous metropolis of London, I didn't feel I belonged anywhere.

To Dorset we certainly belonged, at least Michael did. His family had owned Bryanston for three hundred years. His grandfather and his father before him, had 'reigned' there for nearly a hundred years between them, from 1823 to 1919. By all accounts both in their turn had exercised a benevolent autocratic dictatorship with strong feudal undertones. They enlarged and maintained the estate, cared for their workers and tenants, improving conditions both in housing and agriculture, introduced modern farming methods and provided full employment for all those dependent upon them. They built schools and hospitals, supported and endowed them. They also constantly re-built churches for which today, together with other Victorian landlords, they are often criticised. Granted, their taste may not have been impeccable and as a result of their enthusiasm some ancient treasures may have been lost but their critics might consider the possibility that without their generosity and fervour, many villages today might have only a romantic ruin as their focal point.

Grandpapa's memory was still very much alive when we came to Dorset and he was always spoken of with enormous respect and affection. Even the fact that he had apparently run the Dorset County Council more or less single handed did not seem to be resented although it caused many problems for those who followed his autocratic administration. Whatever his methods, the evidence was clear that he had conducted a very well run Welfare State in miniature.

In the wider world of national government, he had also played his part. He was a member of Parliament for thirty-four years and of the House of Lords for thirty-one. In 1918 King George V, conferred on him his personal order of the Grand Cross. The King's letter asking him to accept this honour and a copy of Lord Portman's reply are still fortunately in the possession of the family.

This unchanging world must have been severely disrupted by the Great War but it did not immediately mark the end of an era.

Grandpapa lived long enough to welcome home the returning soldiers. He did so in style, giving a great dinner at Bryanston for them, men from eight or nine Dorset villages attended it and more important he found work for them. He was ninety when he died after a life-time of being served and giving service to others.

His death in 1919, followed shortly by that of his second son who succeeded him, really marked the end of an era in Dorset. The lands and villages acquired during the nineteenth century had to be

sold to pay double death duties.   This still left the heart of the
estate, the parishes of Bryanston and Durweston, in the possession
of the family virtually intact and back to what it had been in the
eighteenth century.

There was, however, one vital thing missing, a house.   The great
mansion built by the 2nd Viscount replacing the Georgian manor
house, was found to be too big and impossible to staff and maintain
in the changing times of the twenties.   The younger sons, now
middle-aged and settled on their own properties, did not wish to
take on the burden and it was finally sold to become a boys's public
school.   In consequence, apart from the elderly residents of the
dower house in Durwestion, none of the family had lived on the
estate for over twenty years.

Three of Grandpapa's sons had inherited in their turn, all dying
without male issue, before the title and estates came to Gerald my
father-in-law.   During those years although continuing the tradition of caring for and maintaining the estate, they were all, in fact,
absentee landlords.   Michael, Gerald's younger son, although
brought up in Lincolnshire, was no stranger to Dorset.   As a child
he had often stayed with his grandfather and in later years had
hunted with the Portman hounds, of which his father was Master.
Well liked for himself, not only because he was a young scion of
the family, we were warmly welcomed by the villagers and tenant
farmers who made us feel at home immediately.   The 'County' too,
accepted us albeit sycophantically and in some cases slightly reluctantly; Michael had been divorced!   His second wife had to be
tinged with scarlet.

So delighted was I by our new home and with the ties which
already bound us to it that I immediately wanted to find out every
single thing I could about our house, the village, Bryanston and
more about my husband's family who had lived there for so many
generations.   At first my interest was purely personal but very
soon the frustrated historian stirred and I had to record, however
inadequately, for the benefit of Michael's children, who, his elder
brother being childless, were likely to inherit.

Unfortunately, with the sale of the big house, the repository of
the family treasures was lost.   Portraits, paintings, books, silver
and furniture, collected and preserved through the years under one
roof which record and display the history of a family had all been
dispersed.   Many heirlooms had, of course, found a home in the
London house in Portman Square only to be destroyed with the rest
of its contents in the Blitz when it was bombed and completely

burnt to the ground.

Sad as this was it gave me the incentive to search out all I could find and provided me with a hobby which has never failed to interest and excite me. Every picture, map, print, book or scrap of information relating to what I call my Bryanstonia and Portmania became a precious addition to my collection.

My first discovery was the little Georgian church near the site of the original house. Derelict, vandalised, completely forgotten and neglected, it was hidden in the trees where evergreens, dark yews and overgrown laurels ensured its privacy throughout the year. I found it one day, on a walk with the children. The surrounding iron fence was intact, as was the gate, heavily padlocked. That was easy to climb over into the little churchyard where tall nettles and weeds concealed ancient grave stones. We had to force our way into the church though not through bolts and bars, which might have been easier to penetrate than the tangle of vicious brambles, covering the door, which confronted us.

Inside, rotting box pews and broken pavements greeted our eyes, but the cerulean blue of the coved ceiling was as clear and pure as the day it was painted, and the dust could not hide the beauty of the carved wood forming the architrave of the main door through which we had entered. Over the alter, framed by elegant plaster garlands, the Ten Commandments, inscribed in gold leaf on two dark blue panels, stated sternly what "Thou shalt not," do. Despite the covering of dust and the trailing veils of cobwebs, the beauty and charm of the little church, showed through and even in this derelict state, its dignity was unimpaired.

Enchanted by our discovery, I couldn't wait to get home and tell Michael and also to find out the history of the church. Who had built it and how it had fallen into this parlous state. Whilst waiting, as usual for the children who had somehow managed to disappear in three different directions, I studied the marble plaques on the walls. Without exception they were all memorials to members of the Portman family. The earliest, flanking the alter was in memory of Henry William Berkeley Portman who died 19th January 1761.

Then there were the portraits which my father-in-law asked us to house when Uncle Seymour died and Knighton House was left untenanted for a while. They were among the few pictures rescued from the London house after it was destroyed in the Blitz.

They included Stubbs's 'Tiger' and Gainsborough's 'White Lady', both too big for our house and they were loaned to the Tate

Gallery. Michael and I were only too delighted to give a home to three portraits of his ancestors which would decorate the erstwhile bare walls of our dining room.

These painted images, solemnly regarding us at every meal, became part of our daily life. For me they gradually seemed to come alive as I found out a little about each of them.

The earliest in a beautiful Chippendale frame was of Sir William Portman, Lord Chief Justice of England who died in 1555. I discovered that it was this Sir William who had acquired the Marylebone estate in London in 1553 most of which remains in the ownership of the family to this day. There is a story that it was an asses farm originally owned by a man brought up in front of Sir William for sheep stealing, a hanging offence in those days. It so happened that the Judge's wife had been ordered asses milk for a wasting disease, a residence close to London also being essential owing to Sir William's necessary attendance at the law courts, some arrangement appears to have been made whereby the estate was conveyed to the Judge and the prisoner escaped with his life!

Although this story may be apocryphal, what is certain is that the Judge did acquire two hundred and seventy golden acres on the western outskirts of the City of London in the twenty-fourth year of the reign of Henry VIII. For this, his descendants should be eternally grateful.

Opposite him across the dining room we hung the portrait of his great grandson, another Sir William and the last Portman in the male line. Painted by Kneller, heavily be-wigged and armoured, he lacked the gentle charm of his forebear, causing much argument amongst the children who all preferred to sit at table facing the serene countenance of the Judge rather than the stern face of the soldier. Perhaps they also disliked him for capturing that romantic figure, the Duke of Monmouth.

Over the fireplace we hung Gainsborough's portrait of Henry William Berkeley Portman. He is pictured in the park at Bryanston. Carrying a gun, with a spaniel at his feet, he stands casually leaning on a gate. In the background the house can be seen in the far distance. Unlike the other two, both life size threequarter portraits, this was more a landscape, the figure in the foreground, part of it but incidental. To me it was a portrait of Bryanston.

19 Henry's great improvements

"FROM PIMPERN we went over another down to Blandford, and at the descent two piers are very judiciously placed, opposite to Mr. Portman's house, which I shall have occasion to mention, and is in a bottom on the other side of the river, and would not otherwise be observed from the road, tho' it is famous for one of the most beautiful terraces in the world." . . .

"On the 7th I went a mile to Brianstown, Mr. Portman's, originally a Berkeley, but has estates by inheritance with the Portmans and Seymours from the present Duke of Somerset's family, which two names he bears. It is a large el-shaped building. The right side is a good pile of two stories handsomely adorned, with round pillars of the Dorick and Ionick order; the other part is lately new cased in the modern way. It is situated on the river, which by art is made to form an island, near which is a delightful lawn and plantations; from this there is a gentle ascent for a quarter of a mile, to a high natural terrace which extends near to Blandford, and is almost three-quarters of a measured mile long, being a beautiful hanging ground. About three-quarters of it towards the house is so broad as to have clumps of evergreen and flowering plants on the side which is towards the road, with winding and cross walks through them. That end is very steep, and the whole hanging ground is planted with trees and shrubs and is most charming . . ."

This description of Bryanston written in 1754, is from Dr. Richard Pococke's *Travels in England*.

Throughout his life Henry continued to beautify his house and improve the estate. On the former he spent large sums of money, to little avail it seems, for though the exterior impressed the passing traveller, the interior remained inconvenient and comfortless which Gibbon, the historian, was to remark upon when he visited Bryanston in 1760.

Possibly learing a lesson from the house, when it came to renovating the church, Henry did not hesitate to pull most of it down and rebuild it on the same site. It stood close to the Manor House and was in bad repair having suffered neglect through the vicissitudes of the Civil War and the absence of a Lord of the manor for some years. It was small and full of monuments and memorials to the Rogers family who had owned the Manor previously. In 1662 there were only six households in the parish; by the eighteenth century the population had increased considerably.

Henry's new church, with its classic pillared door case, pediment and Venetian windows, was simple and charming. The interior beautifully decorated with plaster mouldings and fine wood carving, was completed in 1745. Beneath it a vault was constructed, awaiting in due course, Henry and his descendants. No trace of a Rogers memorial remained. The walls of the church were bare and ready to receive the memorial tablets of the Berkeley Portmans.

The first marriage to be solemnised in the new church was that of Henry's sister Laetitia to Sir John Burland of Stock Gaylard, near Lydlinch in 1747. It was a relief to Henry to see her safely married at last when he had almost despaired of getting her off his hands. Independent, wilful and arrogant, she had turned down several previous offers of marriage and was thirty-seven when she finally succumbed to Sir John who was fourteen years her junior. Nevertheless she produced a son for him and was to outlive her husband by three years.

Another concern of Henry's was to close or divert the many public highways which encircled and criss-crossed his property. This was to take many years, requiring Acts of Parliament to achieve. Henry made some progress but it was not finished in his lifetime.

These roads are clearly shown on the hand-painted map of Bryanston made by William and Margaret Bowles in 1658. One road from Blandford to Durweston crossed the river by foot-bridge and ford close by the house and continued through the farm homestead, 'nicely described in one document as Mr. Portman's backside.' This road, Henry did succeed in obtaining the necessary powers to close in 1755, but they were not implemented till much later.

The map also shows the boundaries of Bryanston and the adjacent parish of Durweston with which it marched on the north-west. The latter is indicated as 'Sir Robert Coke's land.' The Cokes of Norfolk, later to become Earls of Leicester, were absentee landlords and it was understandable that Henry wished to acquire this estate and extend his own. He was foiled in his objective when the Earl of Leicester sold it to Julines Beckford of Stepleton in 1753. It was left to Henry's son to fulfil this wish, which he did when he finally bought the property from Julines' son Peter Beckford twenty years later.

Henry, however, did have a foothold in the village. He discovered from old family papers that the 'dwelling house and messuage' he had repaired and renovated for Sarah, had been owned in 1550 by Alice Portman, mother of the Lord Chief Justice, Sir William Portman. This unimportant little property had remained in the possession of the family, forgotten for two hundred years before a use was found for it.

He visited the village often and as the years went by his son accompanied him and became friendly with the Godwin boy. Henry William, as an only child had few playmates and Benjamin was in a similar situation, living with this Mother and Aunt in Durweston. Both boys were over cosseted by their mothers and took a great delight in escaping together to fish in the river and ride in the woods and on the hills, from where they could see for miles across the countryside and even, on a clear day, could glimpse the distant sea. They spent many hours with Josiah whose tales of his sailing days enthralled them both. Stories of far away lands, strange people and stranger customs as well as of the excitements and dangers of life before the mast.

At an early age, Ben announced his intention of following the family tradition and going to sea, but if young Henry ever had any such ambition he knew very well that it could never be fulfilled. His future was already planned and determined for him. As the sole heir to the estates in Somerset and Dorset it would be his life long responsibility and duty to look after them. He might become a Member of Parliament, he told Ben, when they seriously discussed their futures. That would take him to London which, from his father's stories, sounded quite as strange and exciting as Ben's 'old sea'. He would build a house there, he said, with all the confidence of a 10-year-old. 'A fine house in a park,' for did they not own property just outside London. It was only a donkey farm but situated conveniently close to the City of Westminster.

20   Henry William succeeds

HENRY WILLIAM BERKELEY PORTMAN, Lord of the Manor of Bryanston and of Orchard Portman, died in 1761 leaving a not entirely inconsolable widow, great sadness in a small household in Durweston and a large fortune to his only son.

Since his marriage, Henry's life had been devoted to his country estates and the sporting pleasures it so amply provided. He hunted and shot over it and entertained his friends lavishly at the Manor. Hard drinking and gambling was the order of the day, and Henry indulged in all these pursuits with the same enthusiasm as most of his friends. Fortunately, as regards gambling, not to the ultimate extent of losing his property on the turn of a card or the fall of the dice as many gentlemen did at this time; sometimes staking an entire estate on one throw at the end of a losing session.

Henry's dedication to his estates no doubt curbed such irresponsibility or possibly he was lucky.

In his last years he had become known as the 'Swearing Squire'. He lived in the period and in the county which was the setting for the novel *Tom Jones*, published in 1749. Henry and his neighbours way of life, customs and manners, must have been similar to those depicted so brilliantly by Henry Fielding in his book.

Edward Gibbon, the historian, who visited Bryanston frequently whilst on militia duties, comments in his diary of July 1760: "The Gentlemen of the County shewed us great hospitality particularly Messrs. Portman, Pleydell, Bower, Sturt, Jennings, Drax and Trenchard, but partly thro' their fault and partly thro' ours that hospitality was often debauched".

With a large rural 'Empire' to maintain, Henry did not attempt to develop his London property, although the Cavendish estate adjoining was already well built up. The revenues from some thousands of acres in Somerset brought in an income more than adequate for his family's needs. The idea of going into the business of property development in the Metropolis was totally alien to his life as a country squire and landowner.

He took great care to see, however, that his son was properly educated. At the age of twelve, young Henry William was sent away to Eton, where he probably learned more sophisticated manners and a wider outlook on his life than in the small world of Dorset.

Travelling was hazardous in the mid-18th century before the Turnpike Trust was formed. The roads were atrocious and long journeys were undertaken only when absolutely necessary. Another danger was the 'Gentlemen of the Road'. On one occasion Henry William's coach bearing him back to school was attacked near Maidenhead Thicket. He was robbed of his pocket money and his boxes cut off the back of his conveyance. The story of this exciting incident must have given him great pleasure to relate. It was passed down through seven generations to my sons, my husband having been told the story by his grandfather, who was the great grandson of the Eton schoolboy.

Henry William was only twenty-two when his father died. Edward Gibbon evidently liked the young man but the comment in his diary about him was fairly astringent. It does serve, however, to give a thumb-nail sketch of Henry's character:

May 29th, 1762
"We were all mortified with the route. It was for Southampton and probably for the Forton duty, as it is usually done from that place. I immediately went up to Bryanstone to acquaint my father with it. Mr. Portman and his mother expressed great regret at it, and indeed our acquaintance with the family was the most to be valued as it seldom can be expected. She is a very good sort of woman. As to him, his good qualities, good nature, generosity and honour are his own, his faults, ignorance, and quickness of temper belong to his education, which was that of a spoilt child heir to six thousand a year. It is only to be feared that his love of fox hunting, hatred to London, and court of dependant persons, may in time reduce him to the contemptible character of a mere country squire. His place (on which and the House) his father laid out £25.000 is delightful. His cliff is the side of a hill about a mile long laid out with GREAT TASTE, cut out into a thousand walks, planted with great variety, and a river running at the bottom. The house is large and well fitted up, but inconvenient and ill-furnished. The prospects beautiful but confined. The other gentlemen of the County, though not so intimate with us as Portman, behaved with great civility to us."

Though the assessment of Henry's character sounds as if it were made by a much older man; Gibbon was, in fact, barely two years older. Nevertheless, his view of his friend is not surprising as he, himself, was entirely different. A scholar and an intellectual who was to become an eminent writer and historian and whose ideas and way of life was totally opposed to those of an English country squire.

His worst fears for Henry William however, do not seem to have been realised, the young squire must have conquered his hatred of London for on coming into his inheritance he immediately proceeded to develop the Marylebone estate, necessitating many visits to London. He did not build himself a fine house on his donkey farm, he leased the land for the building of hundreds of houses, streets and squares. Before he died, a large area around Portman Square, its 'centre point' was built up and inhabited by the nobility and aristocracy and had become one of the most fashionable and sought after residential quarters of London.

Portman Square was planned and laid out and building first started on the south side where a house was mentioned as early as 1765 as having been bought by William Lock, the famous connoisseur and patron of the Arts. Lord Scarsdale and Lady Home were installed in adjoining houses of which Lady Home's was the largest, thus setting the fashionable tone of the Square before it was half completed.

The houses were designed to the individual requirements of the clients by the speculative builders, Abraham and Samual Adam, no relation to the famous brothers. It seems however that Robert Adam had a hand in the design of Lord Scarsdale's house and also supplied interior designs for other residents.

Meanwhile the east and west sides of the Square were rapidly being built up in a more uniform way. The north side was the last to be built. Here too Lady Home acquired the lease of one of the largest plots in 1772. It must have been very convenient for her to supervise the building and decoration of what was to become one of the finest Adams' houses in London, from the other side of the Square.

The mansion across the north-west corner, standing back from the road in its own grounds, with an enclosed driveway in front, a large garden, coach house and stabling for twelve horses at the rear, was built for Mrs. Montagu by James Athenian Stuart and decorated by Angelika Kaufman.

Mrs. Montagu secured the lease of this huge plot in 1773 with every intention of out-doing the Countess of Home, in which in size and grandeur she succeeded, even 'the faultless elegance of her architecture' was approved by Horace Walpole, 'who went to sneer but was surprised into praise.' 'Instead of vagaries, it is a noble edifice,' he reported. He went on to say he thought it a magnificent house. 'It is grand not tawdry, not larded and embroidered and pomponned with shreds and remnants.'

Lady Home had been installed in her house just across the road for some years before Montagu House was completed in 1782. Whereupon Mrs. M. proceeded to outshine her rival in every possible way. Starting with a house-warming breakfast for 700 people, she continued to entertain in this sumptuous style and to attract the rich, the famous, the intelligentsia and the Royals to her salon.

In what was then very much a man's world it seems surprising that the two grandest and largest houses in the square were built for and each occupied by lone women. Lone, of course, only in the sense that they had neither husbands nor children. The number of servants and other employees under each roof would undoubtedly exceed by far the number of people residing in a 'Stately Home' today, even with a large family. Both ladies were widows, extremely rich, socially ambitious and in their different ways equally extraordinary.

Mrs. Montagu has gone down in history as the original 'Blue Stocking,' and friend of Dr. Johnson. By all accounts she was a plain woman. Her wit rather than her beauty was her passport to success, no doubt greatly helped by her money. Fanny Burney, the novelist and diarist, described her as 'brilliant in diamonds, solid in judgement, critical in talk' and as a member of society, 'magnificently useful'.

Her salon was noted for the eminent intellectuals who regularly attended and for good conversation rather than social chit chat and card playing in which her rival hostesses indulged. She was well over fifty years old when she started building her great house in the square, where she lived and entertained until she died in 1800 aged eighty.

One of her eccentricities was to lay on an annual dinner for the chimney sweeps of London. Every May Day, any sweep who cared to come to Portman Square was invited to eat roast beef and pudding on the lawn at any time in the afternoon of that day.

Charles Kingsley's book, *The Water Babies*, is said to have been inspired by the story of a small boy who having been sent up into the chimneys of Montagu House, as was the custom, lost his way in this labyrinth and finally descended into Mrs. Montagu's bedroom. This confrontation with the pathetic sooty child aroused her concern and was the reason for her continued interest in the welfare of such children. The annual sweeps' party which resulted excited much publicity and together with Kingsley's *Water Babies* was instrumental in finally getting this horrible practice abolished.

She also had her frivolous side. She conceived the idea of collecting from her friends feathers of every sort and kind, from peacocks to common cock feathers. These she had mounted and framed to be hung upon the walls of her boudoir until they were completely covered. The Feather Room remained intact until the house was destroyed in the Blitz in 1940.

Mrs. Montagu never ceased tormenting and vying with her neighbour, Lady Home, whom she dubbed 'Queen of Hell'. However, perhaps the Countess had the last laugh after all, as her beautiful house, now the Courtauld Institute, still exists today. The one remaining jewel in the square which, in the golden age of elegance, was the crown of the Portman estate in Marylebone.

William Beckford, author of *Vathek*, who also lived in the square, described Lady Home as an even more extraordinary lady than her rival, Mrs. Montagu. His account of a musical evening at her house, written to a friend, is a long list of criticism of her taste, judgement and manners, bordering on the libellous. Mentioning that she 'swears like a trooper' and is known to the chairmen and riff-raff of the Metropolis as the 'Queen of Hell', he goes on, 'As her infernal magesty happens to have immense possessions not only, as of course, in the realms below, but in the Island of Jamaica, which some think next door to them, she took it into her extremely eccentric head that as a West Indian potentate I ought to receive distinguished homage and determined to celebrate my accession to Portman Square.'

Lady Home, born in Jamaica, had inherited a large fortune from her father, William Gibbons, a West Indian Merchant. She first married the son of the Governor of Jamaica, James Lawes, who left her a widow in her early twenties. She was nearly forty before she married again, this time to the 8th Earl of Home, who deserted her within a year.

Vain, extravagant and by all accounts not the most charming or congenial of characters she was indomitable in her social aspirations. Her two brief marriages had brought her little joy and no children but at least she had acquired a grand English title which must have been a great help. Her house, which she started to build when she was seventy years old brought the beau monde to her door and is probably the only reason she is known of today.

Whilst all this activity was going on in London, Henry William did not neglect his Dorset estate or the consolidation of his family.

Leaving the business in London mostly in the capable hands of his agent and friend, Peter Baker, after whom Baker Street was named, he was free to spend much of his time in Dorset, enjoying the country life he preferred and devoting himself to the essential task of starting a family.

In 1765, Henry William married nineteen year old Ann, daughter of William Wyndham of Dinton in Wiltshire. By her he had five children, two boys and three girls. The growth of his family was more rapid than his property development. All five children were born long before even Portman Square was completed. This slow progress may have been partly due to the Building Act of 1774 which set much higher standards inevitably causing delays and also to the fact that the fine architects of the day, Adam, Stuart and Wyatt, all concerned in the building of the north side, were busy with country house commissions at that time. There was a building boom following the end of the Seven Years' War.

Henry William, commissioned James Wyatt to build a new house for him at Bryanston. The old Manor house had finally become too inconvenient and old-fashioned for his growing family. He pulled it down completely and built the new house on the same site.

The Wyatt house, sadly, was only to survive for little more than a hundred years. Paintings, prints, a ground floor plan and photographs taken in the late 19th century together with a description of the main rooms is the only information we have about it today.

Meanwhile the Bryanston Estate had grown considerably. In 1767 Pimperne and France Farm were purchased by Henry William from Thomas Baker and in 1774 Durweston from Peter Beckford, both adjoining properties, thus more than fulfilling his father's wishes.

He did not realise his own boyhood dream of building a house of his own in London, but at least had the consolation of knowing that his descendants would have the pick of the grand houses in Portman Square when the leases expired and they reverted to the family.

Henry William was not given the name of Berkeley; his father, born a Berkeley, having taken the name and arms of Portman obviously felt that his son, as the first of the new dynasty, should bear that name alone. However, Berkeley was given to Henry William's sons as a second christian name, a custom which is now traditional for all male members of the family.

Henry and Ann's first child was a girl, Ann Mary. Two years

later a son was born together with a twin sister. They were christened Henry and Henrietta. No doubt the parents having firmly
decided on the family name, Henry, for their second child in the
hope that it would be a son and heir, could think of no other name
for this unexpected addition so gave their daughter the feminine
equivalent.

In 1771 a second son was born, Edward Berkeley, followed in
1775 by a third daughter, Wyndham. With two sons the continuation of the family was at last fairly well assured. Though Henry
William, like his father before him, did not live long enough to be
doubly reassured by the birth of a grandson.

During the time the Wyatt house was being built, Henry William
was fortunately able to rent the Down House, virtually next door in
the parish of Blandford St. Mary. The dwelling house on this
property, previously a farm, had been rebuilt on a grand scale by
Thomas Pitt, brother of William Pitt the Prime Minister. His son
Thomas, who inherited in 1761, found his father's affairs in such
confusion and disarray that although he continued the improvements on the Down House estate, decided finally to lease the house
and make his own home at Boconoc on his Cornish property.

The house was rented to Mrs. Portman in 1777 so very conveniently served not only to house Henry William's family
temporarily but also to provide a Dower house for his mother.

The young family moved into their new home in 1778, Henry and
Ann were both in their thirties with five children aged between
twelve and three years old. An idyllic family in an idyllic house?
Through the mists of time that is how it looks and as indeed it may
well have been, there is no evidence to the contrary.

Henry William had to ride to London on business more often
than he wished but these journeys were mostly confined to the
summer months when the roads were less hazardous. In the winter
he was able to indulge his passion for hunting under the best
possible auspices, for over the river at Stepleton lived Peter Beckford who kept the finest pack of foxhounds in the country. Julines
Beckford had bought the property from Thomas Fownes when the
latter had almost bankrupted himself through his single-minded
devotion to the breeding of foxhounds. Beckford, coming from the
West Indies had little interest in this most English of country pas-
times, but his son Peter with all the opportunities for hunting every
sort of game in the Cranborne Chase, grew up to be a keen sportsman as well as a gentleman of intelligence, wit and charm. His
book *Thoughts on Hunting*, published in 1781, was to become the

Huntsman's Bible.   This then was Henry William's near neighbour, the same age as himself and sharing his sporting tastes.   In later years the Portmans had their own pack of hounds and many are the tales of quarrels and feuds with neighbouring Masters, usually concerning the boundaries of the country over which they hunted. However, in those early days, I like to think that Henry William and Peter were friends and enjoyed together the sport that Peter provided in the beautiful Dorset countryside.

21   Into a golden age

THE VILLAGE of Durweston had changed little since medieval times
when Henry William acquired it in 1774.   An ancient settlement
mentioned in the Doomsday Book, its origins were undoubtedly
very much earlier.   Across the river, Hod, an Iron Age hill-fort and
later a Roman encampment, dominated the valley; proof enough
that there had been settlements on the river banks below in prehis-
toric times.

In the eighteenth century there was no longer a Manor House in
existence.   The cottages were clustered near the Church which
stood on rising ground and also lined the village street leading
down to the river and the Mill.   There were two farm houses, one
close to the church and near the site of the ancient Manor Close of
Knighton, once a separate entity which had merged with Durweston
in the fourteenth century.   The population of the twin villages,
decimated by the Black Death, could no longer support two
churches and in 1381, St. Eloi's on the river bank was pulled down
and the two parishes united in the Church of St. Nicolas.

The other farm house was on the Durweston side of the road
which ran from the river ford straight up the hill through the
farmlands and had marked the old boundary between the two
parishes.

The main highway from Blandford to Sherborne via Bryanston
ran right through the centre of the village, passing the church and
both farm houses.   On the corner where it diverged from the village
street stood an oddly named Inn, 'The Blackamoor's Head', a good
house boasting a yard and stabling for a few horses.   The passing
traveller was well catered for, the last house to the west of the
village was 'The Sign of the Gate', the Godwyn's Inn, aptly named
as it was situated near to where the gated road climbed up out of the
valley towards Sherborne.

Small though it was, Durweston was an independent thriving
community.   Surrounded by water meadows, good pasture for
their cattle was assured and the dry chalk uplands provided excellent grazing for sheep and for the growing of grain.   Game
abounded in the woods and on the hill and if it all strictly belonged
to the Lord of the Manor, keepers could not be everywhere and
were certainly out-numbered by cottagers who poached on the

preserves in order to provide extra food for their families. On the common land most were able to keep a cow or a goat and in their gardens as well as growing vegetables it was possible to keep a pig and a few chickens. Wood for fuel was plentiful in the coverts and there for the gathering.

It was as well that they were very nearly self-sufficient for, though there was employment on the farms for some, the weekly wage for a farm labourer varied between 1s. 6d. and the princely sum of 9s. 6d. Cottage rents were around one pound a year.

The Mill was probably the most important asset of the community. For the farmer, small-holder and cottager, it converted the fruits of their labour into an end product which provided income and their staple food.

It was to the Mill that Henry William first turned his attention when he became Lord of the Manor. Recognising that the miller was of major importance to the village, he immediately proceeded to have a new house built for him. Consisting of two good rooms on either side of an entry hall with bedchambers over, it was tacked on to the existing Mill cottage which became the kitchen offices of the house. The upper floor was reached by an elegant staircase, its balustrade designed in the Chinese Chippendale manner. When it was finished in 1776 it was the finest house in the village.

This was but one of the many improvements which Henry was making on the Bryanston property. With the acquisition of Pimperne and Durweston, its size had more than trebled and all his interest seemed to be centred on this estate where he had been born and had made his principal residence.

The birthplace of his father, the Manor of Pylle in Somerset, belonged to his Uncle Edward Berkeley until he died in 1774, when leaving no male heir it passed to Edward's sister Laetitia for her life. She spent her last years as a widow there and on her death it reverted to the male line of her family represented by Henry William, her nephew.

This property, when it eventually came to him, seems to have held little interest for the Squire of Bryanston, though he and his sons were the last remaining descendants of this branch of the Berkeleys. It remained in the possession of the family, however, and was eventually to provide a living for more than one of his grandsons who took Holy Orders.

With the very much larger estates in Somerset from whence the Portmans originated, Henry William had really no personal ties at all. By a lucky accident of fate, his grandfather had inherited them together with all the Portman possessions through the Will of his kinsman, Sir William Portman, but preferring Bryanston and his own house at Pylle, he had never made his home at Orchard Portman.

Born and brought up at Bryanston and now established with his family in his new house, there was really nothing to attract Henry William to the old Portman residence near Taunton. The Manor house was even more ancient and inconvenient that the one he had pulled down in Dorset. In addition, for reasons unknown at the time, there appeared to be a sickness connected with the house. The servants were constantly ill and members of the family had suffered from fevers which in some cases proved fatal. Sir William, the last of the family to reside at Orchard Portman, had lost no less than three wives. It is possible that the unhealthy reputation of the house was one his reasons for living mostly at Bryanston during his last years. If he had planned to live there permanently with his third wife, Mary, and beget the son he so longed for, he left it too late, for Mary too died at Orchard Portman.

In spite of Henry William's preoccupation with Bryanston, the Somerset estates were not neglected. They were valuable possessions and a major source of revenue. Situated in a neighbouring county and no great distance away, the farms and other properties, some of which had been in the ownership of the Portman family since the fourteenth century, were well established and could be efficiently looked after and maintained by stewards and agents answerable to Henry William on his regular though infrequent visits. More land continued to be acquired in Somerset as well as in Dorset through the years. It was said that Henry William's grandson Edward, created Baron Portman of Orchard Portman in 1837, could ride from Blandford to Bristol on his own property. This he actually did annually, on horseback, taking with him his agent to note down all repairs and improvements needed on every farm he visited.

It was he who bought Hestercombe in 1872, probably the last property to be bought in Somerset and the first to be sold when, after enormous death duties, the estates started to be broken up in the 20th century.

For the aristocracy, the great landowners and even the smallest country squire, the 2nd half of the eighteenth century was a 'golden age'. It was a hundred years since civil war had disrupted and ravaged the country and Oliver Cromwell's Commonwealth had cast a gloomy shadow over England. The abortive Stuart rebellions were almost forgotten and the Hanoverian Georges sat firmly on the throne of England.

The word Georgian has become synonymous with beautiful. Georgian country houses in their parklands; terraced town houses in their squares; Georgian silver, furniture and porcelain need no further adjective. Even the landscape was changed and coaxed into new shapes and forms to enhance its beauty. The course of rivers moved, lakes, waterfalls and grottos artificially contrived. Clumps of trees planted on hilltops and steep bare slopes clothed with a variety of vegetation making a mosaic of colour and form through all seasons.

The landowners had the ideas and the money to have these works carried out and their taste was usually impeccable. Architects, cabinet makers, silver-smiths and landscape gardeners; craftsmen in every field prospered on the commissions they received, as indeed they deserved to, for the beauties they created, designed for the few, are universally admired and enjoyed today.

The workers and the poor received little benefit from this extravaganza at the time. They had no voice and their fate was entirely in the hands of their employers and landlords.

Human nature being what it is, some exploited them to the full caring nothing for their welfare. Nevertheless, a social conscience was awakening in England and many landlords administered their estates very fairly, caring for the employees and dependants beneficially, albeit autocratically. The evidence of public service and of the excellent administration of their estates by Henry William's descendants throughout the nineteenth and into the twentieth century is well documented and remembered. There can be little doubt that Henry William too was a man who cared for the welfare of his workers and tenants.

With the passing of the Poor Laws, every parish was required to take some responsibility for their own impoverished parishioners. An annual rate was levied from the more prosperous householders in the community and the money thus raised was used to help the aged, infirm, the sick and needy. It also paid for the upkeep of a Poor House, even in a small village like Durweston. This particular social service, starting off with the best of intentions, was later in the 19th century to become notorious under the inappropriate name of the Workhouse or the Union. They were situated in the towns where paupers and orphans of the town and from the surrounding villages were incarcerated and condemned to a life of misery in many cases.

In Durweston there were seven rate payers in 1792, the highest rate paid was 14s. 3d.—the lowest 2d. From 1773 to 1802 Benjamin Godwyn, Henry William's boyhood friend, was the overseer of the poor. His rate book, beautifully kept, reveals how the money was distributed. Small as the total sum appears today, it seems to have gone quite a long way. It bought blankets for the aged and infirm, paid the rent of those without means, thatched their houses, paid the doctor's bill, bought shrouds for children and paid for their burial. It is interesting to note that two blankets bought for 'old Vinson' at 5s. 9d. was more expensive than the cost of thatching two cottages for the sum of 5s.

Henry William's ambitious schemes to improve his property created employment for many and there was work, apart from agriculture, for most of the able-bodied men in the villages. His plans to close roads running through his property, all too close to his house, necessitated the making of alternative highway, which undeterred, he proceeded to do. The road from Blandford to Sherborne via Okeford starting from the south side of Blandford Bridge, ran up the hill following the course of the river and skirting the back of the Manor house. Here it bore off to the west leaving the horseway to Durweston to continue more or less alongside the river northwards to that village. Henry William's solution to this unsatisfactory state of affairs was to build a completely new road from Blandford running parallel to the old, but starting some four hundred yards further south of the bridge. It finally joined the old highway well past the Manor House. This was perfectly acceptable to westbound travellers and indeed, no doubt, an improvement but it still left the road to Durweston circling his house at which point it was joined by yet another road from the Milldown, which crossed the river by footbridge and ford close by.

Henry William overcame this problem by building a bridge at Durweston to connect up with the Blandford-Stourpaine highway on the other side of the river. This was not as simple as it might have been for the road here ran over high ground and therefore had to be diverted about a mile back, down to the bridge, and had to continue up a steep hill again to Stourpaine.

On the Durweston side the low-lying water meadows flooded constantly so the new road into the village had to be carried over them on six sturdy arches. The powers to achieve all these changes took over ten years to obtain and necessitated an Act of Parliament, Henry William having to prove that the distance from Blandford to Durweston was no further on the other side of the river than the original route on the west bank through his park.

The old road from Blandford to Durweston was closed to the public and became the private driveway to the Manor House. A fine arched gateway and lodge was built at the entrance by Blandford Bridge and a high wall along the entire length of the new road separated it from the grounds. At Durweston, the drive, diverging across the meadows to the new bridge, thus by-passing the village, was closed by gates flanked by twin lodges. The Cordon Sanitaire was finally complete.

At Bryanston the clutter of farm buildings on the river bank, which had grown up around and served the old Manor through the years, were all pulled down and rebuilt on the other side of what was now the private drive. Out of sight, screened by plantations of trees, the barns, wagon sheds, forge and carpenter's shop, together with a farm house and cottages formed here a model village catering for the needs of the big house and housing its employees.

Only the elegant stable block, built at the same time as the church by Henry William's father, remained conveniently adjacent to the house. The formal gardens on the south side were swept away as was the bridge over the river, now unnecessary. The new house stood in isolated splendour looking over parkland with the river winding through it.

A GLIMPSE of life in Dorset, when Henry William's children were growing up at Bryanston, was to be found in a collection of letters and diaries belonging to Anne Catherine Bower, a friend and neighbour. Written between 1780 and 1796 they present a vivid picture of social customs and domestic life in Dorset at that time. They make fascinating reading, concerning as they do the everyday events and occupations of these Dorsetshire families.

Fortunately preserved, on being discovered more than 100 years later, probably in an attic, they were published privately by the Bowers family in 1903.

Anne Catherine was born in 1768, her grandfather was Thomas Bower Esquire of Iwerne. As a girl, she lived with her family at Rushmore, which her father, Bower's eldest son, rented from Lord Rivers.

Catherine, as she was usually called, her sister Elizabeth, the three Portman girls and other daughters of neighbouring families were all sent away to school at Mrs. Ivie's in the Close at Salisbury. Here they were carefully looked after, well taught and happy, until they were about 12, when most of the girls went on to Mrs. Stephenson's school at Queens Square in Bloomsbury.

The earliest letter to Catherine is from her headmistress and dated 19th March 1780. Mrs. Ivie expresses regret at Miss Bowers' continued absence from school, wishes that she would not 'loose any time that she could improve to her advantage' and hopes she will 'make up for her absence with double diligence on her return'. After continuing with news of the teachers, compliments to Catherine's family and friends, she ends her letter thus:

> *I am Dear Miss Bowers' most affectionate friend and obliged Humble Serv*
>
> *Mary Ivie.*

The letters from Catherine's family are always full of warmth and affection and when she was at school, concern for her education and improvement. Her grandfather did not hesitate to use bribery to these ends. In a letter promising to send a turkey and other 'goodies' for the Ball and entertainment Mrs. Ivie is planning for

her young pupils, he concludes with advice and a dire warning to
his twelve year old grand-daughter:

> *I am glad to find you think yourself improved in every branch of*
> *your Learning: the fruit that those Branches will produce will*
> *shew the effects of the improvement: indeed you may look upon*
> *the Game, Fruit, and the other presents sent by your Relations, as*
> *one of the Effects of your improvement: for was it to be once*
> *represented by Mrs. Ivie that either of you was careless, negligent,*
> *or inattentive, from that instant all presents of every kind would*
> *cease: and as it is entirely in your own Power to merit the Contin-*
> *uation, I think you are both too wise to risk the forfeiture and*
> *consequently the loss of them: I shall conclude with this Piece of*
> *Advice: Continue to Deserve and you shall both have everything*
> *you Desire, that is in the power of*
> > *Your affec: Gfather*
> > *T. Bower*

Mrs. Ivie's pupils were taught the art of letter writing and
encouraged to correspond with each other which they apparently
continued to do for many years. They were all neighbours as well
as school friends and had everything in common. They detailed
their activities minutely to each other, the balls, races, visits in
town and country; commented on the health of the King [George
III] and on the Napoleonic Wars; gave news of family events and
gossiped about their friends in Dorset, providing a window into the
daily lives of these country families two hundred years ago. These
people were, of course, the privileged few, taking their happy situation in life totally for granted. Not surprisingly, as between themselves it was never questioned, and those who might have done so
were simply not within their orbit.

Amongst letters from schoolboys, requests for servants refer-
ences, and the charming letters exchanged between Catherine and
her fiance always full of fun, teasing and family jokes, there are
three letters from Anne Portman to Catherine:

> *A.M. Portman to Cath. Bower.*
> > *Bryanston, Janry 1st 1791.*
> *Dear Miss Bower,*
> > *We have lately been at Dinton to celebrate Mr. Wyndham's*
> *birthday, who was of age the 18th of last month; We had a*
> *pleasant party in the house [which] chiefly consisted of Uncles*
> *and Aunts, & Cousins. Mr. R. Arundell was there one day; Mr. &*

Miss Arundell were also expected, but were prevented, by having Company at home.   We had a tolerable good Ball at Blandford last Tuesday, about twelve Couples; a great deal of Dancing, did not get home till near three o'Clock, which in my opinion is much too late for a Country Ball.   Mr. Bingham dances as brisk as ever.   Miss Bingham was not there, she fatigued herself too much at the Dorchester Ball the Thursday before.

Mrs. Beckford is extremely ill & Mr. Beckford has written to Mr. Rogers, desiring him to send Master Horace to Italy with all possible speed, as Mrs. B. wished very much to see him.   I am very much afraid from this account that she is in a dangerous state.

What dreadful weather we have had lately, my Brother, who is but just come from London, says there was a great deal of damage done there by the late tremendous winds, no doubt but you must all have been very much alarmed, as I believe most people were that heard it.

Mrs. and Miss Sturts are at Critchell, & Mr. Fox, the Marquis of Blandford & a large party of the Salisbury family.

We shall I believe go to London the middle of February for three months.   I hope by then to be able to write you longer letters. Dorsetshire does not at present abound with news.

All the family have desire to join with me in best Compliments to yourself, Mrs. Bower, & all the rest of the family, wishing you all many happy Years—
I remain,
Dear Miss Bower,
Your ever Affectionate Friend,
ANNE MARY PORTMAN.

Henry Seymer, Esq., to the Rev. W. Blandford.
Alresford, Febry 13th 1790
Dear Blandford,

I got a good calves Tail the other Day, & have made up three Baits for you, and ordered the Butcher to save me the first red one he can meet with & then I shall make up the rest of your Hooks.

Our servant Wm is going to leave us, & as I remember you spoke well of some of your Abraham's Brothers, if you think any one of them would be likely to turn out a good, clever, sober lad, willing to learn the NOBLE Science of waiting at Table, & make a good Mercury, I shall be much obliged if you will dispatch Him to

me by Mr. Gibbons; he will have Liveries found Him and every-
thing commonly given to Footmen, & as for Wages, such a Lad
could not at the utmost reasonably expect more than six Pounds a
Year.   If none of these should be likely to answer my Purpose, &
you should know anyone else, that would suit me, for you perfectly
know what Wm has to do, I wish you to Converse with him &
dispatch Him to me by the same Conveyance, if you can agree to
the terms; if he knows how to Catch up a Horse & saddle Him, &
can ride without being tied on, it will be all the better.

I have not killed anything this great while, & probably shall not
go out any more.

    With best Respects from my little Woman
              I am
              Dr. Blandford
              Sincerely your's
              HENRY SEYMER.

        Anne M. Portman to Cath. Bower.
            Bryanston, Febry 1st 1791.

Dear Miss Bower,

I find your sister Elizabeth is certainly to be married this
month, pray give my love to her & tell her that I hope whenever
she comes to Dorsetshire, she will not forget her friends at Bryan-
ston, as they will at all times be happy to see her.

Several Dorsetshire families go to the GREAT METROPOLIS *this*
week; the Richard's, Damers, Pitts, Bakers, & the Portman
family go the beginning of the next week to stay about four
months.

A very curious AFFAIR *has lately happened at Milborn, at Mr.*
Pleydells, there is in that House a Bedchamber hung with
Tapestry; some Company who were there on a visit lately, for one
night only, amused themselves with cutting the Eyes out of all the
Figures in the Tapestry, & likewise the Tails of the Beasts, the
ornament off the Top of a Glass was taken down & thrown into
the Fire, the best ends of the Poker & Tongs were likewise put into
the fire & entirely spoilt; they also took the trouble of moving the
Draws into the middle of the Room, & turned them down the
wrong way & several other things as SILLY, *it must have been*
merely for mischief sake.   This is the common subject of conversa-
tion all over Dorsetshire & it was told at this House at Dinner
before eighteen People & likewise before all the Servants. Let me

know what you think of this RIDICULOUS STORY in your next letter. The families in Dorsetshire will I believe take particular case, how they ask any of the party that was concerned in this affair to their Houses. I do not think they have many friends in this County, & they were much too old to behave in this Childish manner.

Reprehensible as was this deed of vandalism, Anne Portman's account of it makes her sound a little priggish and lacking in a sense of humour. Catherine Bower's attitude was quite different, recounting the story in a letter to the Rev. William Blandford, her husband to be, she says how much it made her laugh, although, of course, deprecating such behaviour! In a later letter from London with some caution, Anne reveals the names of the miscreants.

Anne Mary Portman to Cath. Bower.
February 28th 1791. Harley Street.
Dear Miss Bower,

We have been in London about a fortnight very few of our Dorsetshire friends have come to town. Mrs. Richards & family have a house in Dover Street, we have spent several very sociable Evenings with them, no fuss of dressing, carried out Work, staid Supper, Bread & Cheese & Porter. My Father is not yet come to town, we expect him the middle, or latter end of next week. My brother came last Wednesday. As you wish to know the names of the destroyers of the Milborn Tapestry I will inform you—the Party consisted of Mr. Ashley Sturt, Mrs. Humphrey Sturt & old Mrs. Sturt's Maid, who was a Player; this is no secret, but (I) beg you will not mention that I told you their names. I believe Ashley Sturt is at present at Winchester School. We went to a large party at Mrs. Sturts in St. James Square last Tuesday, a great deal of fine company, the Prince of Wales, Duke of York, & Clarence were there, & Mrs. Fitz Herbert who look'd very handsome. Lady Archer was also there, who look's exactly like an enamel's Doll. Indeed I must say I never saw such a disagreeable looking figure, she disguises herself so with White Paint & Red. There was a large Party at the Faro Table; & there is another new Table brought up, called the Rouge & Noir, game, I hear Mr. S.L. is to be the Dealer, & to be PAID so much an hour for Dealing, people who have seen the game play'd say it is something like Faro, only you have a Chance of losing your Money much quicker. I believe we shall go to the Opera next Tuesday, which will be over about eleven o'Clock, & from thence to Mrs. Sturts Party.

Last Thursday we went to a Play at Covent Garden, "The School for Arrogance", the entertainment, "Patrick in Prussia". The most fashionable Play this Year, is the "Siege of Belgrade", it is acted at Drury Lane, the House is very much crowded every time it is acted, I have not seen it. The fashions this Year are not much altere'd, as to Caps & Bonnets: the deep veils which some people wear are FRIGHTFUL, *I have a very moderate one, & find mine* EXTREMELY TROUBLESOME, *I hope this year will be the last of wearing them, everything is made very high and narrow, the fashion Colors are Coquelicot & Pistache. Heads are dressed very narrow, & flat at the Sides,* EARS *are in fashion now. So much for this nonsense—I saw Mrs. Baker last week, she was very well, & is at present very busy furnishing her new house in Portman Square. This morning we have about thirty Visits to make, a very unpleasant employment, merely* FORM, *& wishing not to find any of the people at home, nothing so troublesome as getting in and out of a Coach every ten minutes. I've not heard any Dorsetshire news worth communicating to you. Pray let me hear from you soon. My Mother & my Sisters desire their Compts and best love to your sisters, & I remain*

Yours sincerely,
A.M. PORTMAN.

The following charming invitation was from Lord Rivers to the newly married Catherine and her husband William Blandford:

Lord Rivers to Mrs. Blandford.
Rushmore to Farnham.

Notwithstanding all the Benefit of this Rain, Rushmore laments that it is just now kept from Farnham, as the Lodge did propose to visit the Cottage this Evening. If on the other hand, the Cottage will favour the Lodge to-morrow, and bring its Night Caps, it will be the kindest & best of all Cottages.

If the weather be tolerable, a morning Visit to Ranston is meditated for to-morrow. The Richardses are there & Ld Rivers was much press'd to dine there, but he said NAY, *& intends being at home by four, or half after to dinner, if that hour should be convenient to Mr. & Mrs. Blandford.*

Should they kindly agree to all this, no answer will be wanted, as the Messenger is a Passenger, Should they unfortunately say NAY, *they must be at the trouble of sending that ugly Word.*

P.S.—How clever it would be if Mr. & Mrs. Bower should chance to be at the Cottage, & would be of the Party!

Sunday Evening
The Lodge. Sept. 17th 1791

A typical request for a reference, Catherine seems to have had some domestic trouble in her cottage at Farnham:

Mrs. Clavill (Senior) to Mrs. Blandford.

Mrs. Clavill presents her respects to Mrs. Blandford, requests to be informed if Pamela Fudge be strictly honest, sober, cleanly, and of a good temper. Mrs. C. understands from the Young Woman that she has lived a year with Mrs. Blandford & left her place on account of some disagreement with the other Servant.

Manston
Tuesday 23rd Augst

Cath. Bower to the Rev. W. Blandford.
Bryanston Monday Night.

I told you I would write you a line this Evening & you see, my dear Blandford, I am as good as my word, though as you desired to hear all the news, I shall comply with your wishes & not finish this till tomorrow morning.

I have a favour to beg of you which is to give me the two first Rails you kill. Mr. Portman is remarkably fond of them, Mr. Wright sent two here to-day & he was toasted even by the Ladies for his present after Dinner; I daresay the same compliment will be paid to you. I am to go fishing to-morrow. they all say I shall catch Jacks. I wish I may. I shall equal you then. Mr. H. Portman gives up a days shooting to go with us: we are to have a Boat & be quite in stile.

Only Lord Delawar here besides the Family—we had some music to-night; he plays a little upon the Violoncello. I think he is more beautiful than ever.

Mrs. Portman says I have stolen her earrings but I assured her they were given to me.

I am going to net Mr. Henry Portman a Waistcoat, we talk of going tomorrow to choose the Colors.

It is between twelve & one, I must go to Bed or I shall not look blooming enough to be complimented on my looks to-morrow, as I was to-day. I believe every Body in the house but me is asleep, as I suppose Old Man is; Cath: wishes him a good night.

I hope you will get this before you set off for Rushmore. Too wet a day I fancy for Fishing. I shall finish this after Breakfast for now I am in a hurry to dress myself, being en Robe de Chambre & just out of Bed, and here they breakfast early on account of sporting. Mr. Portman says there are not any Birds & neither he nor his sons have any sport.

We have just finished Breakfast. Mr. Portman & Lord Delawar are gone shooting. We are all going to Wimbourn to buy bargains. The rain in the night has prevented our fishing. Adieu, Old Man.

Life appears to have been one long round of entertainment for the young with balls at the Assembly Rooms in Blandford, Shaftesbury and Dorchester and dances in private houses. 'Company weeks' when the house party stayed not for a weekend but for a fortnight or more. Each small town had its own theatre; favourite plays at this time were *The Rivals* and *The School for Scandal.* Riding out and card-playing were daily occupations and the Race Meetings at Blandford were grand social occasions.

23   Edward B. Portman MP

HENRY WILLIAM died in 1796 aged fifty-seven. In his comparatively short life he had accomplished most of what he set out to do. He left the Dorset estate in excellent order, enlarged and improved. The Marylebone estate was almost fully developed up to and beyond Marylebone Road. This was London's first by-pass, its purpose being to relieve the congestion in Oxford Street caused by cattle driven up to Market from the west. A small area in the centre of the property, still open fields, was already planned and laid out for more residential development which was to include Bryanston and Montagu Squares.

He had been High Sheriff of Dorset and had served in the Militia. Although he had never found time to enter politics, both his sons were already Members of Parliament, Henry for Wells and Edward for Borobridge.

Henry William's major ambition to ensure the continuation of the family however was still unfulfilled. His eldest son, married for three years, had not yet presented him with a grandson. Happily, before he died, he knew a baby was on the way and did not live long enough to suffer the disappointment of this child inconsiderately electing to be a girl.

Henry William was laid to rest in the vault of St. Martin's Church at Bryanston next to his father. A second marble plaque went up on the wall to commemorate him, facing one he himself had erected to his parents. His own memorial was very much larger, leaving space, not only for his wife, but also for those of his children whose names in future years were to be inscribed on it.

When the mourning was over life at the manor went on much as before. His widow and three daughters remained in residence. The girls appeared in no hurry to marry, possibly they enjoyed their life at Bryanston too much to wish to change it. Of the three only Henrietta married and then not until she was thirty.

Two years after his father's death, his younger son Edward married Lucy, daughter of the Rev. Thomas Whitby and a year later a son was born to them. The birth of this child was the cause of great joy to the whole family. It was almost as if it was acknowledged that Henry would have no more children and that the future of the family might depend on this baby.

More than a hundred guests were invited to the christening party which followed the child's baptism in the church built by his great-grandfather. The entertainment to celebrate the event was on the most lavish scale and went on all day and into the night. There was dancing in the Library and cards in the Music Room, the sumptuous buffet was described as looking too good to eat and the guests were hesitant to sample the master-pieces of culinary art so exquisitely contrived by the pastry cooks. The centre piece of one of the long tables was a model of Durweston Bridge spanning a river of jelly complete with swans drifting upon it.

The raison d'etre for this extravaganza was described by a guest, who wrote a long and detailed account of the proceedings, as a 'sweet and beautiful child who regarded the scene with evident intelligence and approval'.

The boy was named after his father, Edward Berkeley, and indeed had every reason to be a happy and contented baby, surrounded as he was by loving parents, doting aunts and a little girl cousin to play with. It was to be many years before he realised that Charlotte Fanny, his Uncle Henry's daughter, came to bitterly resent the fact that she was not able to inherit the house they all loved. During his last illness, when a very old man, he declared that she haunted Bryanston. ''Tis only Cousin Charlotte, not to worry', he reassured the frightened nurse who had seen a ghostly white figure in his bedroom. It is said that the 'White Lady' still walks on the green grass beside the Church where the Wyatt house once stood.

Henry William's eldest son died aged 35 in 1803 and Edward inherited the estates in Somerset, Dorset and London. The latter had considerably increased in value owing to the urban development, making a transition from farmland to something more like a gold mine.

By this time, Edward, already had two sons and with every intention of further increasing his family, he found it inconvenient for his three maiden sisters to remain in residence at Bryanston. Mompesson House in the Close at Salisbury was leased for them and here they set up their own establishment. This beautiful house was to be their home for the rest of their lives. Henrietta married L.D.G. Tregonwell but often returned to visit her sisters after she was widowed. A room in the house is still known as the Rocking Horse room. I was a little confused when informed of this on visiting Mompesson House, wondering why the elderly Portman sisters required a room in which to 'stable their rocking horses'. A little research soon provided the answer. Evidently it was kept as a playroom for Henrietta's three little grand-daughters, Henrietta, Wyndham and Mary Tregonwell, when they visited their grand-mother and great-aunts, after whom they were named.

Edward, having dealt with these family matters and his duty to his dependants, could then turn his attention seriously to politics. Times were changing; England was at war with France and the Industrial Revolution was well under way. The lesson of the French Revolution and conditions which had led up to it, not so very different from those pertaining in England, had shaken the politicians and slowly brought about changes in their attitudes. Some MPs, like Edward Portman, began to think more seriously about reforms and of improving conditions for those less fortunate than themselves. Both he and his brother had secured their seats in Parliament through money and privilege with little personal effort, but far from wishing to retire from politics when he inherited Bryanston, Edward's ambition was to represent his Home County.

In 1806 he stood for Dorset against Bankes, and after a particu-larly bitter and acrimonious campaign, won the seat which he held for the rest of his life.

In London he continued the development of the Marylebone estate, though it was slow during the years of the Napoleonic Wars. Bryanston and Montagu Squares were built between 1810 and 1815. These were leased to a developer, David Porter, reported to have been 'Chimney Sweeper' to the village of Marylebone. Chimney sweeps seem to have done rather well in this part of London, maybe he had been a protege of Mrs. Montagu, perhaps that very child who had appeared in her boudoir, making his unconventional entrance via the chimney. It is a nice thought.

Of the two new Squares, Bryanston was the grander and more elegant with ionic columns adorning the centre and end houses on each side of the Square. The architect for the lay out and facades was Joseph Parkinson, a young man influenced by Robert Adam's idea of planning an urban terrace of houses to look like one large building or palace.

At home Edward sought to improve the conditions of his employees. His terrace of seven cottages in Durweston backing onto the new road leading to the bridge, was a model housing project in the days when Dorset labourers were notoriously badly housed. They were brick built and tiled, each with three bedrooms above the living quarters. At the bottom of the gardens, inside the walled complex, every cottage had its own spacious work shed and

a pig sty in addition to a discreet row of earth closets,
'conveniently' situated as far as possible from the terrace.   In each
garden was planted an apple, a pear and a plum tree to complete the
amenities.   Later, the luxury of piped water was laid on to stand
pipes along the path in front of the cottages and a brick built
communal laundry was built for the use of the residents.

Model cottages indeed in the early nineteenth century, though
not by today's standards.   Nevertheless, they remained exactly
the same, including the rent of 6d. per week for over one hundred
and fifty years; always maintained by the estate in good repair;
they housed large families, sometimes more than one.

Today with electricity and water laid on to each house, they are
sold and snapped up as bijou residences by newly married or
retired couples, who open up the inglenook fireplaces, install a
bathroom in one of the bedrooms and are happy to pay a price for
each, far exceeding the original cost of building the whole terrace.

Edwards' wife, Lucy, duly presented her husband with two more
sons and three daughters before she died in 1812.   Left with seven
children between thirteen and one year old, Edward suffered a
devastating loss, but much as he needed a substitute mother for
these infants, he did not marry again for some years.   Finally, in
1816, he married Mary, daughter of Sir Edward Hulse of Breamore
and the children acquired a step-mother.

Once more the family was complete, but it could not be the same
as in the halcyon days of his first marriage or of his own happy
childhood at Bryanston.

In 1823 he fought his last election, once more against Bankes, it
was a campaign as bitter as the one he had fought 17 years before,
and in the midst of it he died suddenly on a mission to Rome.   Like
his father and grand-father before him, he did not live to see the
birth of an heir in the next generation, but with four healthy sons,
this could not have been of such concern to him as it had been to his
predecessors.   Regretfully, he never knew that his eldest son was to
be persuaded to take his place and continue to fight the election
against Bankes.

Young Edward was a reluctant candidate.   At first he agreed but
then changed his mind.   Only after much pressure he finally
accepted and won the seat with a large majority, to the great joy of
his late father's constituents.

24   *The first Noble Lord*

EDWARD PORTMAN was 24 when he succeeded his father.   At this early age he found himself head of the family, responsible for three brothers, the youngest still at school, and three sisters.   In addition he had the considerable family estates to manage.   Having been reluctantly pushed into politics, he was also M.P. for Dorset. Educated at Eton and Christ Church, Oxford, where he took a B.A. degree, becoming an M.A. five years later, his qualifications were probably as good as those of any young man of his time, nevertheless the heavy responsibilities thrust upon him by his father's early demise must have been fairly testing.   Fortunately two of his sisters were soon married.   The eldest, Lucy Mabella, was betrothed to G.D.W. Digby of Sherborne within a year of her father's death, and married him in May 1824.   The youngest, Harriet Ella, married William S. Dugdale of Warwick three years later, both were in their teens.   This left only Marianne dependent upon him, who far from being a burden, took over the running of his household, their step-mother having departed to London, and eventually provided a companion for his young bride, during the first years of his own marriage.   Marianne finally married George Drummond of Stanmore, Middlesex, in 1831.

Edward could have had little time for his own amusement or the sowing of 'wild oats' so it was as well that he was a serious young man dedicated to his family and proud of his lineage.   He was descended in the male line from Robert Fitzhardinge to whom Berkeley Castle was granted in 1153 by Henry II.   His ancestor Maurice was the younger brother of Thomas Berkeley, Lord of the Castle when Edward II was murdered there in 1327.   This horrific event is not something any family could be proud of, but in mitigation, history does suggest that Thomas was only a pawn in the hands of Edward's enemies, and had no direct responsibility for this dastardly deed.

It is from this Thomas that the present owner of Berkeley Castle is descended.   The Barony and later the Earldom of Berkeley were conferred on the senior branch of the family in the 15th and 17th centuries respectively.   These titles are now dormant or extinct, for collateral branches descended from the earlier Barons, who held title by tenure not writ, could not inherit them.

By the mid nineteenth century, the Berkeley Portman line was immeasurably strengthened. In 1827 Edward married Lady Emma Lascelles, third daughter of the Earl of Harewood. He was twenty-eight and his bride eighteen. Their first child, a son, was born two years later. After this comparatively slow start, for a child must have been most anxiously awaited, Emma made up for it by presenting her husband with three more sons and two daughters in rapid succession. With the birth of her youngest son, Walter, in 1836 the family was complete for though Emma was only twenty-seven she was to have no more children. In the meanwhile, Edward's three younger brothers all married and in due course produced sons. Very soon there were many more lines springing from what, for so long, had been a single thread. Fragility was a thing of the past.

Perhaps it was as well that the nursery at Bryanston was so well filled in those early years of marriage for a major change in their family life was on the horizon.

In 1837 only weeks after her accession to the throne, the young Queen Victoria invited Emma to be one of her ladies of the Bedchamber. Emma's acceptance of his honour was to entail long periods of absence from Bryanston. Spells of duty in London, first at Kensington Palace, later at Buckingham Palace and also at Windsor, meant that more of her time was spent attending the Queen than in her own home with her husband and children. A letter to Edward starting "My Own Beloved", clearly shows how much she missed her husband and family.

Emma was probably well aware of the sacrifices she would have to make but the invitation extended, in a friendly and charming letter by the Queen, must have been difficult to refuse. Emma attended Victoria at her coronation and later was Matron of Honour at the Queen's Wedding.

Before Victoria came to the throne, in the last months of William IV's reign, Edward was raised to the peerage with the title Baron Portman of Orchard Portman.

Unlike Emma's appointment to the Royal Household a few months later, this honour caused little change in their lives. Nearly 200 years of Squiredom lay between Sir William Portman, the last Baronet and Edward Berkeley Portman, the first Noble Lord, but such is the mystique and power of titles that it would appear to many that the family 'started' in the 19th century with the first Baron Portman. It is true, however, that he ensured through his sons, its continuation. In the family tradition, Edward's main interest was in his country estates, the administration of which he pursued with even greater enthusiasm than his forebears.

His heart was never in politics, and having dutifully represented Dorset in Parliament for nine years in the moderate liberal interest, he gave up in 1832 to devote himself to the improvement of agriculture. His special interest in cattle breeding was shared by other landowners in the West Country and resulted in the creation of a new strain known as the Devon. Exported in large numbers to South Africa and Uruguay, the breeding of these animals won for him many awards. His model farm buildings at Websley on the hill above Durweston Village, was a show place to which farmers and landowners flocked to view the revolutionary and modern methods he had instituted for the rearing and management of his Devon cattle.

The buildings still stand in isolation on the hilltop, not abandoned for the farmer finds many uses for the well-built barns and yards—but no longer used for their original purpose. Below in the valley, huge prefabricated iron barns and byres have taken their place.

In the 1860s leases of the first houses in Portman Square were starting to fall in. The sites bought in the eighteenth century by speculators and individuals, were all on a ninety-nine year lease. They built their houses on the land they acquired, and thereafter paid only a peppercorn rent to the landlord. When these properties reverted to the estate they could be leased again on very different terms, vastly increasing the landlord's income from them. Henry William's 'crop', though taking a hundred years to mature, reaped a rich harvest for his descendants.

When the lease of Mrs. Montagu's house expired in 1872 Lord Portman promptly took it over for himself as his town residence which had previously been in Bryanston Square. The name, Montagu House was dropped and it became simply known as 22 Portman Square.

The first Viscount's youngest grandson, Gerald, was born there in 1875. In the event, he was to be the first, last and only member of the family to be born at 22, a fact which seems to have given him some strange satisfaction. Remarking on it to his son, Michael, after the house was razed to the ground by enemy action in 1942, he added ambiguously, 'now no one else will be born there, it's probably just as well!'

Edward lived a long and very full life. His appointments included, Councillor of the Duchy of Cornwall and of the Duchy of

Lancaster. He was a founder-member and President of the Royal Agricultural Society and Lord Warden of the Stanneries. For twenty-five years he was Lord Lieutenant of Somerset, from 1839 to 1864. In 1873 he was created Viscount Portman of Bryanston. His loyalties were always divided between Somerset and Dorset. It is interesting to note that when first made a Peer, he dutifully took the title of Baron Portman of Orchard Portman from whence came his name, but with the second creation he adopted the title of Vis. Portman of Bryanston, the place where he and his forebears were born, where his heart really lay and to which he had devoted* his considerable creative and practical talents.

25   The passing of an era

WILLIAM HENRY, 2nd Viscount Portman waited a long time before he succeeded his father, unlike his predecessors, all of whom had inherited in their twenties, brought their brides to Bryanston and raised their families there.

In 1855 William married Mary Selina Charlotte, eighteen year old daughter and only child of Viscount Milton, heir to Earl Fitzwilliam.

Knighton House in Durweston provided a suitable residence for them to start their married life, his father having already considerably enlarged the old farmhouse which was in a secluded and delightful situation no more than a mile or two from Bryanston. In the event this was to be their home for more than thirty years for the old Lord lived to be nearly ninety. At Knighton William and his wife brought up nine children; six sons and three daughters. As the family grew the house proved to be too small to accommodate them comfortably and a temporary wing was added. Not until the 1880s was piped water laid on so it is not surprising that an enormous number of servants were required and employed, nor that it was considered small for a family house of that period whilst today as a girls boarding school it houses a hundred pupils.

William served a long apprenticeship but was not idle during those years. In 1854, aged twenty-five he was elected Member of Parliament for Shaftesbury and remained a Member until he succeeded to the title and went to the Lords. He was a conscientious and serious politician, active in local affairs too as well as helping to administer the family estates. When his father died in 1888, three of William's children were already married. The second Viscount moved into Bryanston House with his wife and the four youngest children: Susan Alice, aged twenty-two, Seymour twenty, virtually an invalid, Gerald, the youngest son, only thirteen and Mary aged eleven. The oldest daughter Emma was married to the Earl of Leven and Melville.

Three sons were settled on their own estates. Edward, the eldest, had Hestercombe in Somerset, which his grandfather had acquired in 1873, no doubt to replace the old family house at Orchard Portman which he had demolished earlier. The reason for its destruction is obscure, especially as at the same time he rebuilt the church there. However, it probably had something to do with the unhealthy reputation of the manor house which had persisted through the ages. In his journal of 1857, his son William graphically describes a visit to Orchard Portman. Leaving Bryanston in his own new carriage drawn by 'his Lordship's' horses, he set off for Somerset taking with him his young wife and infant son 'Teddy'. There appear to have been many minor mishaps on the journey of about forty miles which took eight hours. Admittedly they did make a call and visited a church on the way. During their week at Orchard, however, worse was to come.

"Miserable day", William records on 7th August, "Teddy ill with teething." The baby's teething troubles continued for a few days and then on 11th August:

"Mary and all the servants ill with cholera!"

The old house was living up to its reputation.

Harry, the second son, still a bachelor, had Buxted Park in Sussex, an estate his mother had inherited from her maternal grandfather, the Earl of Liverpool. Harry, later married Emma Andalucia Frere, widow of the Earl of Portarlington, by whom he had a daughter.

For the third son Claud a new manor house was built in parkland near the village of Child Okeford.

A family story must have a scandal or a feud and it was Claud who provided both of these ingredients. He married firstly Mary Ada Gordon-Cumming in 1888, who presented him with two daughters, Guinevere and Joan, the latter dying in infancy. The marriage lasted only ten years, was dissolved by divorce and Claud immediately married again. His second wife was Harriette Mary, daughter of William Stevenson, by whom he had a son, Edward Claud, and two daughters. The divorce, a commonplace event today, caused an enormous scandal. The newly married couple were ostracised by the rest of the family who were forbidden by their father to have any communication with them. There is a story that on one occasion, Lord Portman insisted on his entire party leaving the Races at Blandford because Claud and his wife were present. Six carriages, each drawn by four horses, processing away from the course when the races had barely started, must have made the point very clearly. Claud moved out of Dorset.

Lord Portman's decision, shortly after he inherited, to demolish the Wyatt House and build an enormous mansion designed by N. Shaw, on a different site, seems, under the circumstances, rather extraordinary. By the time the house was completed in 1898 he was nearly seventy, all his children grown up and dispersed.

It was said that he was influenced by his wife, Mary, who complained that the manor house, so close to the river, was damp and furthermore, it was too small. The latter may well have had something to do with the fact that Mary's own ancestral home, Wentworth Woodhouse, in Yorkshire was the largest house in England. Perhaps she considered that after waiting so long to take up residence at Bryanston, she deserved a grander house.

These considerations may have partially influenced William, but I am convinced his main purpose was to build the great house for his heirs and for posterity. He was immensely rich and the succession secure. He could not have foreseen the changes which were to come about so rapidly in the next two decades which were to make it impossible to retain it as a family seat. Today it houses, with additional buildings around it, a larger family than could ever have been contemplated. Six hundred boys and girls, pupils of Bryanston School, their tutors and their families, enjoy the spacious house and beautiful grounds of what has always been a much loved 'place in the country'. Though it did not fulfill its original purpose I feel that my husband's grandfather would have been happy to see the mansion he had commissioned Norman Shaw to build, put to such excellent use.

The explosion of male issue in the Portman family during the 19th century ensured the family's survival. Cousins now abounded, offspring of William's uncles and brothers, where before it had often depended on a single life. Ironically the 2nd Viscount's own direct line proved to be not so secure. Four of his six sons survived him, yet it was to be his youngest son's younger son Michael on whom finally its continuation depended.

Michael, born in 1906, married twice and had two sons, Edward and Michael William. He did not live to inherit as his elder brother, Gerald, twice married but childless, outlived him by a few years and it was Edward who succeeded his uncle in 1967. Michael was fond of his grandfather and admired and respected him enormously. In October 1919 the old man died aged ninety. It so happened that Michael was with him at the time. They had travelled down from Scotland together, the aged Viscount and his youngest grandson aged thirteen. Making an overnight stay at 22 Portman Square, grandpapa announced that he was a little tired after the journey and would not stay down for dinner. Asking for a tray to be sent up to his room he retired early and Michael, looking in to bid his grandfather 'goodnight' might well have been the last person to see him alive. The grand old man went to sleep and did not wake again.

Appendices

Queen Victoria's letter of 6th July 1837, from Kensington Palace, inviting Lady Emma Portman to join the new monarch's Ladies of the Bedchamber:

My dear Lady Portman,

      Having had the pleasure of being personally acquainted with you for some years, and having always had a great esteem for your whole Family, I should be delighted to appoint you one of my Ladies of the Bedchamber. —

If this appointment
suits you, I should
be very glad to see
you here at half-past
three o'clock on Saturday,
and I beg you will
bring my little friend
Ellen with you. —

Believe me always,
dear Lady Portman
your's very sincerely

Victoria R.

Mary Selina Charlotte Wentworth Fitzwilliam, born 1836, engraved by George T. Doo in 1838. [She would marry the second Viscount Portman.]

Bryanston House, built by Sir James Wyatt in 1778. The stables, to the right, still exist and were being restored in 1987 by Bryanston School.

Lord and Lady Portman at the Wyatt house in the 1860s.
[Baron Portman became the first Viscount Portman in 1873.]

The second Viscount Portman. [1829-1919.]

Sir Leslie Ward's "Spy" print of the second Viscount Portman. 'An old master' is the caption – he was master of the Portman Hunt.

Blandford's Market Place in Victorian times.

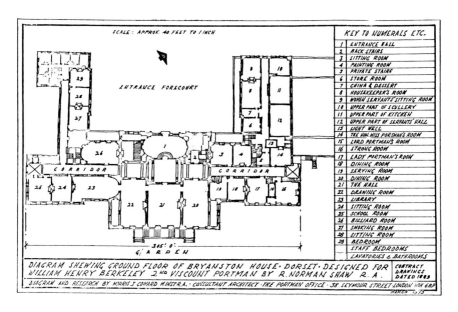

Ground plan of Norman Shaw's new Bryanston House.
[Research: Morris J. Coward.]

Bryanston House, built by Norman Shaw in the 1890s. The Portman Hunt is meeting. Shaw also built New Scotland Yard.

The garden side of Norman Shaw's Bryanston House.

The luxurient hall of Bryanston House.

The ballroom of Bryanston House.

The drawing room of Bryanston House. The picture over the fireplace is
Gainsborough's 'White Lady'. She was Anne Fitch, wife of
Henry William Berkeley Portman.

**The second Viscount Portman's family in the drawing room
of Bryanston House, about 1898.**

St Martin's church, Bryanston. Built in 1898, partly on the site and using the stones of the demolished Wyatt house.

Mompesson House in The Close, Salisbury, was the home of Anne and Wyndham, daughters of Henry William Portman.

St Nicholas's church, Durweston. Drawn by H. E. Portman in 1826.

**St Nicholas's church, Durweston. After rebuilding by the
second Viscount Portman, 1846. Painted by his sister Louisa Mary.**

Lulu was nurse to the second Viscount's children in
Knighton House, Durweston. Painted by J. Evans Eccles.

**Uncle Harry, the third Viscount, was the last Portman to live
at Bryanston.** [1860-1923.]

Letter from Lady Emma to her husband, the first Viscount Portman, in 1837:

BUCKINGHAM PALACE
Tuesday

My own beloved

Here we are arrived and so cold this house is and all the precautions which the Queen had directed to improve it, are not yet finished; my rooms are very comfortable and close to Lady Theresa's. The Queen is in great spirits at coming to Town—I wish you could have seen her last night you would have been charmed; an official Box came just after dinner, she took out her bunch of keys unlocked it, read the contents and wrote the answer with so much calmness and decision and then went to her room where I followed her, and locked up her papers in a most business like way; after she returned she played on the Piano Forte and was as merry again as if nothing had occurred; she is a very wonderful character and so engaging; she enquired for you today very kindly—I hear from the Baroness that the Queen is very particular that all those belonging to her Household should attend either House on great questions and that she watches the Lists; it is therefore very well that I said that it was on account of the cold that you were afraid to come so far when she asked me yesterday if you would be here today—The Duchess of Kent begged to be remembered to you last night—I always wish her out of the way, though she is very kind to me, but I feel so much more at ease with the Queen alone who is really very delightful— The Baroness I delight in too—We walked yesterday through the Court of Eton College into the playing fields which are so pretty; I thought of my boys being there some day or other—Queen Adelaide is ill again spitting blood—I like Colonel Grey very much; he is very merry and gentlemanlike she too is a pleasing person. Shall I see Hardwick whilst I am here and look at any house he may have in view—I will find out Lord Tavistock's address for you by tomorrow's post, today has been all bustle—Tell Ella that her letter is very nice, it had one mistake in the French sentence. Whenever you can get a nice bunch of violets you may send them, the Queen likes a little bunch to stick in her gown. God bless you my own love
        forever

          E. Portman

The correspondence between King George V and the second Viscount Portman conferring upon him the G.C.V.O. [Knight, Grand Cross of the Royal Victorian Order] in 1918:

BUCKINGHAM PALACE

July 11ᵗʰ 1918.

Dear Lord Portman

Within a week of my Silver Wedding you enter your ninetieth year. I hope you will allow me to commemorate these two events in our lives by conferring upon you

the Grand Cross of
my personal Order (G.C.V.O.)

I am anxious to do
this as a mark of my
high appreciation of one
who having lived in
five successive Reigns
has rendered valuable
service to his Country,
& as a great landowner
both in London & in the
West of England, has
given an example of
high minded, disinterested

devotion to duty.

The Queen joins with me in hoping that you may continue to be blessed with that remarkable activity of mind & body which you now enjoy.

Believe me

very sincerely yours

George R. I.

July 12–[19]18
Bryanston
Blandford.

Sir,

I feel much honoured by your Majesty's offer to confer on me the Grand Cross of your Personal order—which I gratefully accept, and shall prize much—but prize still more the kindly expressions towards me from your Majesty, and her Majesty the Queen—and your united good wishes for my health and strength—any services of a Public nature which I have been called on to render, I have always looked on as incidental to the position in which circumstances had placed me, and for which I have never expected any sort of reward, but the honour which your Majesty now confers on me is all the more appreciated—May I be allowed to offer to your Majesties my congratulations on your Silver Wedding, and to express a hope that you will celebrate your Golden Wedding in more peaceful and less anxious times than the present—
With my humble duty, I beg to remain your Majesty's obedient subject, and servant,

Portman

To
His Majesty
The King.

*Pedigree of the Orchard family of Orchard [later Orchard Portman]
near Taunton, Somerset, from 1135 to the fifteenth century when Cristina Orchard married Walter Portman [died in 1475]:*

Azure, a chevron between three pears pendant or, ORCHARD.
Argent, a chevron engrailed between three roses gules barbed vert,
MANINGFORD. *Argent, three trivets sable,* TRIVETT.

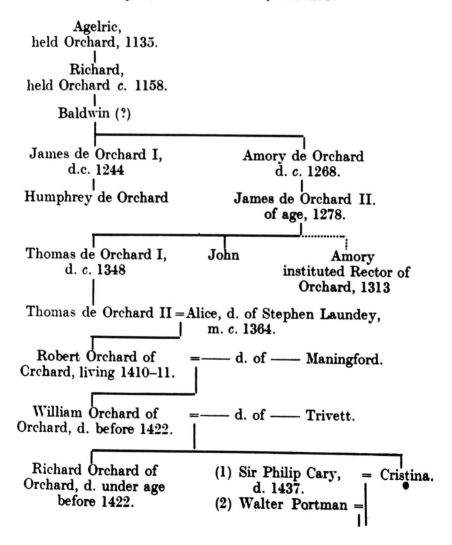

Agelric,
held Orchard, 1135.

Richard,
held Orchard c. 1158.

Baldwin (?)

James de Orchard I,   Amory de Orchard
d.c. 1244   d. c. 1268.

Humphrey de Orchard   James de Orchard II.
                             of age, 1278.

Thomas de Orchard I,   John   Amory
d. c. 1348   instituted Rector of
                                      Orchard, 1313

Thomas de Orchard II = Alice, d. of Stephen Laundey,
                         m. c. 1364.

Robert Orchard of   = —— d. of —— Maningford.
Orchard, living 1410–11.

William Orchard of   = —— d. of —— Trivett.
Orchard, d. before 1422.

Richard Orchard of   (1) Sir Philip Cary,   = Cristina.
Orchard, d. under age   d. 1437.
before 1422.   (2) Walter Portman =

Afterword

GRANDPAPA WAS not buried in the family vault at Bryanston. He joined his wife and children, who predeceased him, in the churchyard of St Nicholas at Durweston.

By this time Bryanston's old church had fallen out of use. It had been replaced by the present church which reuses stone and materials from the house built by James Wyatt. In any case the family vault was full.

In 1957, after being virtually abandoned for half a century, the old church at Bryanston was restored and reconsecrated. The work was carried out by Gerald, the 8th Viscount, with the Portman Trustees, and it became the Portman Memorial Chapel.

All Michael's grandchildren were christened there over the next two decades. Michael only lived to attend the baptism of his first grandson, Christopher, in 1958. There were to be four more sons born to Edward, the 9th and present Viscount. It became clear that the succession of what is still the 2nd Viscount's direct line would no longer hang on that fragile thread.

A·CLEAN·HEART· AND ·A·CHEERFUL·SPIRIT·